GROWING
Vegetables

Mum,

Looking forward to sampling
the fruits of your labour!

Christine xoxo

GROWING
Vegetables

An easy guide for all seasons

Sarah O'Neil

NEW
HOLLAND

First published in 2016 by New Holland Publishers Pty Ltd

London • Sydney • Auckland

The Chandlery Unit 704 50 Westminster Bridge Road London SE1 7QY United Kingdom

1/66 Gibbes Street Chatswood NSW 2067 Australia

5/39 Woodside Ave Northcote, Auckland 0627 New Zealand

www.newhollandpublishers.com

ISBN: 9781869664572

Managing Director: Fiona Schultz

Publisher: Christine Thomson

Designer: Andrew Davies

Production Director: James Mills-Hicks

Printer: Toppan Leefung Printing Limited

10 9 8 7 6 5 4 3 2 1

Keep up with New Holland Publishers on Facebook

www.facebook.com/NewHollandPublishers

Dedication

Whether they chose to or not, I believe everyone should know how to plant a seed and get food. This is a life skill that is being lost. Fortunes can be made and lost in an instant and knowing how to grow food can be the difference between being hungry or healthy.

Thank you to my wonderful family who love and support me in my passion for growing all our food and through all the madcapped projects I drag them through. I am blessed to have you and love you all so much.

A bowl of vegetables

with someone you love

is better than steak

with someone you hate.

PROVERBS 15:17

(NLT)

CONTENTS

INTRODUCTION

Many people feel the urge to grow their own food, yet don't know where to start. Gone are the days where this life skill is passed down through the generations. So the keen gardener is left to find their own way through a minefield of information overload.

This book has been created to guide and encourage you, week by week, through your first year of growing your own vegetables.

❊ It takes growing food back to basics and explains when, how and why to do things.

❊ It has been designed with you, the gardener in mind and how you would logically work your way through the season.

❊ The book doesn't mind being taken into the garden to be referred to when needed.

❊ Taking notes throughout the growing season is encouraged and there is space within the pages and at the back for your records.

❊ It is designed to encourage you to think about your specific garden so at the end of the growing season you can confidently wade through the myriad of gardening information and make informed decisions.

❊ The relaxed, friendly style comes from a place where I want you to experience success and go on to have a long love affair with growing you own food.

Happy gardening,
Cheers,

Sarah. ☺

LATE WINTER

It may be cold and miserable outside and seem like spring will never come, but it is in these early days that the garden really begins to take shape, not in the soil but in the mind of the gardener. Any time and effort put in at this early stage will go a long way towards the success of the garden throughout the growing season. The good thing about this time of year is gardening can be done from the warmth and comfort of indoors without working up a sweat. It is tempting to rush in and start right away. But with gardening everything happens in its own time and now is the time for planning.

Sow	*Plant*	*Maintain*	*Harvest*
• Outdoors – broad beans, carrot, spring onion, parsnip, peas, radish, silverbeet, swede and turnip.	• Plant asparagus crowns.	• Plan and prepare a new vegie bed.	• Broccoli, cabbage, cauliflower, leek, parsnip, silverbeet, spinach, swede and turnip.
• Indoors – beetroot, cabbage, celery, pepper, spinach and tomato.	• Plant garlic, shallot and onion sets.	• Test the soil to see how best to prepare it.	
	• Plant strawberries.	• Dig in generous amounts of compost.	NOTE: This is just a guide – things may happen faster or slower in your garden..
		• Boost existing plants with a feed as the weather begins to warm up.	

Frozen kale.

CHOOSING YOUR SPOT

The first question to ask yourself is: WHERE?

This decision requires a bit of commitment as you may need to give up your sunniest spot, as many summer vegetables require a good eight hours of sunshine. But think of the amazing fresh tomatoes, still warm from the sun, eaten right there in the sunniest spot in your garden. There are rewards for your sacrifice.

Have a good look around. The ideal spot may be sunny right now, but if there are trees close by how will it be in the height of summer when the trees are full of leaves? Tree roots can also be a problem for gardeners as if the tree is very close to the garden, the roots will seek out your richly fertile and well irrigated garden bed and eventually, over the years, completely take over the bed until it is nothing more than a thick mat of tree roots. I've seen it before!

Also make sure there are no underground pipes and cables that will be disturbed by your digging and cultivating as this could be costly and dangerous if you dig one of these up!

A garden should be wide enough to comfortably reach into the centre of or, if it is against a wall, you should be able to easily reach to the back it.

Trees near gardens can be a problem.

The next question is:
HOW BIG?

This is entirely up to you and the space you have available. You could go as big as you like if you have the space and dig up your whole lawn (unless you're restricted by a landlord!). Also, you can grow veggies in containers, and take them with you if you move.

Two metres by three metres is a good size for a first-time garden, not too big that it becomes overwhelming, and not too small that you don't get to enjoy the fruits of your labours.

Raised bed

In-ground garden

Raised Beds vs In-Ground Gardens

Raised beds	In-Ground Gardens
• Great for less than ideal situations like sandy or boggy soil or poor topsoil	• No cost required to create the garden – just a bit of digging effort
• The exact composition of the soil can be controlled	• In most cases the soil beneath our feet is more than suitable to grow food
• The height can be adjusted to suit poor mobility	• The soil retains moisture well
• Provides a physical barrier to the edge of the garden	• Earthworms and other beneficial organisms are already present
• The soil warms up earlier in the season and stays warm longer at the end of the season	• It is easy to extend the garden should you want to in the future

PLANNING AND SPACING

There are three keys to a good veggie garden and that is SOIL, SPACING and TIMING!

First it is important to focus on spacing. It is best to do this before you start growing anything and the best way to do it is by making a plan on paper, in pencil so you can move things about until you are happy with it.

What do you grow?
Well what do you like to eat? You don't need to grow things you don't actually like to eat. Spend some time looking through catalogues, look at the seeds on offer at your local garden centre, look at what your family actually likes to eat. This should give you a great place to start and probably a very long list.

Can I grow what I have chosen?
Deciding what you want to grow is only part of the planning. Once you decide what you want to grow, you have to have a good look at your garden to check you have enough space. You may need to

TAKE NOTE
WHAT IS GOING ON IN YOUR GARDEN THIS WEEK?

How big is your spot? Where does the sun rise and set and is there is any shade during the day? Are there any nearby trees?

Take a photo now because it will surprise you to look back and see how far you have come.

....

....

....

....

....

....

....

reach the hard decision that you can't have everything.

Plants do best in their own personal space and if you squish in too many then you will compromise the harvest … if you get that far. Trust me on this one. Plants too close together are at greater risk of diseases and pest infestations and often fail to thrive.

This is one of the classic mistakes I have seen over and over again. Seedlings look tiny so lots of plants get planted out too close together. There are recommendations on seed packets and seedling labels and they are pretty spot on. The seedlings may look silly in their space in the middle of your garden, but they will grow and fill the space and it will be hard looking back to remember how tiny they were.

HOW TO READ SEED PACKETS AND CATALOGUES

Seed packets and catalogues often have beautiful images making you want to grow it all, however they are more than just packets to hold the seeds or there to make it a pleasant experience when making decisions. These are a value resource and contain a wealth of information.

The key points that you should take from a seed packet or catalogue are:

* Description – this gives you an idea of how the plant will grow and what it will taste like and even some interesting tips.
* Where – does it like full sun or can it cope with a bit of shade? So essentially where you should plant it.

Dates on seed packets are more of a best before – provided they have been stored correctly. But the freshest is always preferable.

* When – this is quite important as if you plant vegetables to early or too late you won't see a harvest.
* Depth – this tells you how deep to plant the seed for best success.
* Germination times – how long it should take for the seedling to pop up. If a few days beyond this, you see nothing emerging from the soil, it may be best to start again.
* Spacing – how far apart you need to plant the seedlings in the garden in order to get the best crop. It isn't just about the parts you can see, but the roots need space too.
* Height – this is especially important if the plant is tall, as it will need support and you need to consider where in the garden it goes so it doesn't get in the way of other plants.
* Maturity – how long it will take to get something to eat. Circle this date in your calendar so you know when to start looking for the harvest from when you sowed the seed.

They should all provide this basic information. You will find some will offer up more information than others but on the whole there will be enough information for you to have a successful outcome.

MAKING PLANS

* The first thing is to draw out your garden, preferably in scale on grid paper or measured with ruler – a 2 metre by 3 metre bed can be represented as 20cm by 30cm.
* Or you could make a grid up on your computer using whatever software you are most comfortable with. There are also several good online programs if you search for 'Vegetable Planner'. You can find a grid at the back of the book on page 209.

Paths between beds should be wide enough for a wheelbarrow or a lawnmower and also a wide enough so you can sit comfortably between the beds while you are tending your garden.

TAKE NOTE
WHAT IS GOING ON IN YOUR GARDEN THIS WEEK?

What vegetables have you decided to grow? Are there any you would have liked but couldn't fit in?

....

....

....

....

....

....

....

....

....

* Mark out where each plant will go – using the correct planting distances and plan it all out. Tall plants like tomatoes, climbing beans and sweetcorn should be put at the back so they don't block the sun from the shorter plants.
* Sweetcorn should be planted in blocks – not rows, for effective wind pollination and full, fat cobs.
* Zucchini is a large plant and can grow a good 2–3 metres if not more, over the course of the summer. It can be planted on the edge of the bed so you can direct it out over the edge of the garden.
* Cucumber can be trained up a trellis or structure or allow to grow over the ground.

When the time is right to plant your seedlings into the garden – stick with the plan. If you unexpectedly find yourself in possession of a plant too good not to have, don't try and squeeze it in, make your garden bed a little larger to accommodate it or pop it in a container.

VEGETABLE SPACING

This is a rough guide for how to far apart you should plant your vegetables in a row.

The more plants in the metre row the closer you can plant the next row and the less plants the wider the gaps between the rows.

One plant per 1 metre will need a one metre gap between rows.

Sweetcorn is best grown in a square patch and not in rows as it helps to grow healthy cobs.

Only plant as much as you have space for.

The growing season should be increased or decreased for warmer or cooler climates. Check out what works best in your local area.

REPRESENTS A 1-METRE ROW

| **Artichoke** | 3 | MID AUTUMN – EARLY SPRING |

| **Asparagus** | 20 | EARLY – LATE WINTER |

| **Beans** | 30 | MID SPRING – MID SUMMER |

| **Beetroot** | 30* | EARLY SPRING – EARLY AUTUMN |

| **Broccoli** | 12* | MID SPRING – EARLY AUTUMN |

| **Cabbage** | 12* | MID SPRING – EARLY AUTUMN |

The number in the middle suggests how many plants a family of four would need in a year, but you don't need to plant them all at once.

The ones marked with a * can be planted at regular intervals in their growing season.

The dates on the end are a guide to the best times to grow the veggies. It is based on an average temperate climate.

| Carrot | 100* | LATE WINTER – LATE SUMMER |

| Cauliflower | 12* | MID SPRING – EARLY AUTUMN |

| Celery | 20 | LATE WINTER – LATE SPRING |

| Cucumbers | 5* | EARLY SPRING – EARLY SUMMER |

| Eggplant / Aubergines | 4 | LATE WINTER – LATE SPRING |

| Garlic | 50 | LATE AUTUMN – LATE WINTER |

| Leek | 40* | EARLY SPRING – EARLY SUMMER |

| Lettuce | 12* | EARLY SPRING – LATE SUMMER |

| Onion | 300 | LATE AUTUMN – LATE WINTER |

| Peas | 60* | EARLY – LATE SPRING & LATE SUMMER – EARLY AUTUMN |

Peppers and Chillies	5	LATE WINTER – LATE SPRING
Potatoes	50	EARLY SPRING – EARLY SUMMER
Pumpkins / Squash	3	MID SPRING – EARLY SUMMER
Radish	20*	EARLY SPRING – LATE SUMMER
Silverbeet / Chard	9	LATE WINTER – LATE SUMMER
Sweetcorn	24	EARLY SPRING – EARLY SUMMER
Tomatoes	12	EARLY SPRING – LATE SPRING
Turnip	30*	LATE SUMMER – EARLY AUTUMN or LATE WINTER – LATE SUMMER
Zucchini / Courgettes	3	MID SPRING – MID SUMMER

WEEDS

Now you have decided where to put your garden you may need to clear a space for it. How you go about clearing the ground of weeds can make a huge difference to the battle you will face with the unwanted interlopers throughout the season.

Probably the most important gardening rule – **DON'T LET WEEDS FLOWER AND GO TO SEED!**

The best way of keeping on top the weeds is to pull them out while they are small. Check your garden every day or so and just whip out anything that shouldn't be there. In a new or neglected patch, a lot of weeds will come up, but persevere and eventually you get on top of them – although you will never get rid of them completely.

Know your weeds

There are some weeds that are easy to eject – just pull the plant up before it set seeds and that is that – that plant won't come back. But weeds don't have their weedy reputation without good reason. There are some real thugs out there. These ones are tenacious and devious and have incredible survival techniques that can become a bit of a nightmare. But knowledge is power and by understanding what makes theses thugs so strong, will also help you to attack them at their weakest.

A common word used to describe these weeds is pernicious and if you care to put it into a thesaurus you will get great words like 'evil, malignant, spiteful and wicked.' So you can sort of see what you are up against. I would not put any of these in the compost heap as they have zombie-like qualities.

A good way to look at weeds is to determine what makes them so difficult to deal with as not all weeds are created the same.

Airborne and Passengers

The seeds that blow in or arrive stuck to the fur of your dog or deposited by berry eating birds. These you really have no control over other than not allowing them to set seed. Examples of these include Thistles and Blackberries.

Creepers

These are the ones that spread across the garden either above or below ground and put down roots wherever they can. For example, Buttercup have a spreading stem and puts down roots at regular intervals. Or Convolvulus which has deep underground stems called rhizomes that grow and spread prolifically in a season sending up new shoots along its length.

Taproots

Many weeds like to anchor themselves firmly into the earth with no intention of

There is an old gardening expression that says "One year to seed; seven to weed." This points out quite clearly that ignoring weeds can make a rod for your back for quite some time.

Thistle

Dandelion

Take some time to examine the weeds in your garden and find out as much as you can about them and what is the best strategy to remove them before you start.

moving. Digging these thugs out can take real effort, but it pays to get it all out as any piece or pieces of root remaining in the soil is able to regrow into a new plant. Removing Dock and Dandelion will give you a great work out.

Bulbils

Not many weeds have this trait, but if you have ever dealt with one you know how much of a pest it can be. These plants have little 'bulbils' at the base of the stem where it meets the roots. Each bulbil has the ability to grow into a new plant, but they don't hold on to the plant very well and so as soon as you tug at it to pull it out of the ground the bulbils fall off like rats fleeing a sinking ship.

As you will be able to pick up most of these thugs have common ways of clawing their way into your garden. And knowing what makes them indomitable will make it easy to develop an effective strategy to get rid of them, instead of just digging over your patch chopping up roots and stems willy-nilly and disturbing seeds and bulbils and making things worse.

DON'T BE TEMPTED TO USE A ROTOVATOR IN YOUR NEW GARDEN, *it may seem to be the easy option but in the long run what it can do is chop up the roots of nasty weeds that only need a part of a root to grow. It also awakens dormant seeds and generally spreads weeds about. So what will happen is during the first couple of seasons you will have made a rod for your own back.*

A GUIDE TO GETTING A WEED-FREE GARDEN

Excluding light

Cover the garden in cardboard, newspaper or a thick mulch. The aim is to block out the light so the plants can't photosynthesise and so they can't make their energy and so they go yellow and then die. Grass and most of the weeds should be killed in 6–8 weeks under the cardboard, then any stubborn weeds, which will be significantly weakened, can be removed by digging them out. Don't use plastic or weed mat as it is just nasty and not good for the soil in the long term.

You really don't want Dock seeds to spread

Manual labour

Mark out the area of your garden and grab a spade or a garden fork and just dig. Cut the soil with a spade in small manageable chunks, about a spade depth, and pry it out and turn it over. If the soil is loose, you can shake the weeds out. If it is damp and it is a bit difficult then leave it upside for a few days to dry out. The tops of the weeds will be mostly buried and so will be weakened. You don't need to do it all in one day.

Environmental

Often it is the environment that the weeds love and so by changing the conditions in the garden you make it less desirable. For example, buttercup enjoys wet, poorly drained soils.

Chemicals

Most weeds respond to treatment with sprays and chemicals and there are many on the market targeting specific weeds. Make sure you choose one that is suitable for vegetable growing areas and follow the instructions.

Sheet Mulching

Natural solutions

I would offer a word of caution here, as there are many suggestions out there for 'natural' remedies to your weed problem, but can often cause more harm than good by changing the acid balance of the soil, killing all the beneficial microbes or causing salts to build up in the soil. Do your research.

IMPORTANT: DON'T DIG SODDEN SOIL!

If your soil is very wet or waterlogged, digging and even just walking on it can destroy the soil structure and it can take seasons to recover. You will compromise the quality of your harvest!

What to do with stubborn weeds not suitable for the compost heap:

❋ Solarisation – put them in a black plastic rubbish bag and leave them in the sun and bake them until they are dry and crispy. Leave them a bit longer to ensure they are really truly dead and they should be good to go on the compost heap.

❋ Weed soup – Place them in a bucket of water and leave to soak until they begin to rot and give up their nutrients. Then drain off the liquid, dilute 1:9 with water and feed to your plants. I must warn you it does stink!

❋ Or throw them in the bin and let the rubbish truck take them far, far away.

It's not advisable to put weeds with seeds on your compost pile. A home compost system is not big enough to destroy the seeds and you could end up with a bigger problem.

WHAT IS GOING ON IN YOUR GARDEN THIS WEEK?

Which weeds do you have? How will you get rid of them?

UNDERSTANDING SOIL

Many gardeners are stirred into action by the first warm day and head off to the garden centre and grab everything they want to grow, hastily clear the beds of any weeds, throw in all the plants and hope for the best. However, this can be a recipe for disaster.

To achieve a bountiful harvest from a healthy garden it is important to get the soil right first. There is no set formula for making good soil as it is all different. Take the time to understand your soil and find out what kind of soil it is and what it needs. Then do what it takes to make it its best. This will make all the difference in the long run.

**Here is a basic question for you:
What is soil?**
It covers all the dry bits of the earth, and we walk all over it without giving it a second thought.

For gardeners there are about five layers of interest. Beyond these are rock and even further down earth's core and magma but we don't really need to know about those.

The layers we need to know about are:

To ensure the best quality food from your garden, it is important to really understand what is going on in the soil you will be growing in. Poor soil will result in poor quality food, however nutrient rich soil will give you nutrient rich food.

Mulch
This is the organic matter lying on the top like lawn clippings and fallen leaves. Gardeners can recreate this natural layer by adding it to their veggie gardens to retain moisture and suppress weeds – although beware as this layer is an awesome hiding place for pests such as slugs and snails.

Topsoil
This is the part plant roots call home. There is a lot going on here. Earthworms bring organic material down from the mulch layer, break it down and deposit it in a form more accessible to plants. There are also loads of bacteria and fungi which love rotting organic matter and create bi-products plants can use. The plants and fungi are also great mates and the fungi can help roots to absorb nutrients more efficiently.

Topsoil also has inorganic matter – minerals and fine particles from the rock below it. There are many different kinds of rock and as a result there are many different kinds of soil. The organic matter and the inorganic matter work together to give the soil structure, drainage and the all-important nutrients.

Wait for the soil to dry before digging.

Subsoil

This is the layer below the topsoil. It is mostly inorganic matter and has more in common with its rock origins. You don't really want to incorporate this into your growing zone, however it can determine features of your garden, especially drainage. A clay subsoil can mean a boggy topsoil, and a sandy subsoil and result in a dry garden that holds very little water.

Water table

This is the level below the surface which the water in the soil normally sits. It will increase with rain and decrease in drought, but generally it has a level that it is normally at during each season. This will impact soil drainage and your irrigation needs.

It is helpful to retest every year or so, to see how much it improves over time.

And so that is what your soil is essentially made up of. All you need to do is figure out how good the soil in your garden is!

SOIL TEXTURE

A quick and easy way to tell what kind of soil you have is reminiscent of preschool mud pies. Take a representative sample of soil from your garden – several scoops from different places from the topsoil layer – about a spade's depth and give it a good mix. Grab a handful of this soil and moisten it and knead it until it is a soft pliable ball. Then roll it out into a sausage and try and bend it into a circle. If it feels soft and smooth and makes a perfect circle, then you have a clay soil. If it feels gritty and cracks instead of bending, then you have sandy soil.

* High Clay – can be improved by adding loads of organic material, manure and compost. Drainage can be helped with some sand or pumice and the clay can be broken up with a little lime. It is also best to create ways to avoid walking on this soil so it doesn't become compacted, by incorporating paths, stepping stones or making the beds narrow enough for you to reach into.
* High Sand – can be improved by adding loads of organic material like compost and manure. This will help provide better water retention as this is quite poor in sandy soils.
* Loam – this is the best kind of soil, however you have to work with what you have – or you can build a raised bed and fill it with a lovely loam soil.
* You should test your soil at the start of each season as the addition of organic matter and harvesting of crops can alter the soil over time and you could have improved or diminished soil quality at the end of the season.

Good soil.

What kind of soil do you have? What is the pH level? Do you have many earthworms?

....

....

....

....

....

....

....

....

....

....

....

....

....

EARTHWORMS

Worms love a healthy soil and the more the merrier. Check your soil quality by taking an earthworm survey. Take the soil from a hole about 20cm square and about 20cm deep and search for worms. Count them up.

More than 10 = good soil.
Less than 5 = adding organic matter will greatly improve things.
0 worms = very poor soil. You have a lot of work to do to make it rich and worm friendly.

pH

This is a measure of acid and alkalinity. Most veggies like to grow in soil that is between 6.0 and 7.5 which is neutral, leaning towards slightly acidic. Like in all things, there are exceptions, so you also need to find out what your plants actually like.

You can pick up a soil test kit from your local garden centre to test a representative sample of your soil. Adding a little lime can reduce the acidity. Adding sulphur can increase alkalinity in the soil. Don't overdo it though – less is more. Follow the instructions on the packet carefully, as it is much harder to undo overzealous adjustments.

✷ Acidic soil makes the nutrients too soluble and they will wash away.
✷ Alkaline soil binds the nutrients tightly and the plants can't get at them.

WHAT ABOUT THE NUTRIENTS?

This is another detail that you need to understand as most of the additives such as compost and fertiliser display nutrient information on their packaging as a way of rating the nutrient quality of the product.

NPK is a phrase bandied about by knowledgeable gardeners, but it isn't some

Sand (top), loam (left) and clay (right).

kind of secret code. It is the chemical symbols for the three key nutrients plants need to thrive.
* **N:** Nitrogen – This generally comes from organic material and great for healthy lush foliage, big leaves and strong shoots.
* **P:** Phosphorus – A mineral from the soil that helps plants grow strong roots.
* **K:** Potassium – A mineral found in the soil and helps with plant reproduction especially fruit, flowers and seeds.

These are the three main nutrients but there are about nine other nutrients plants need to thrive. However, N, P and K are the main ones by which most compost, fertilizers and additives are rated.

Some of the other minerals that your plants need are:

SECONDARY ELEMENTS
* Calcium – essential for building strong cell walls.
* Magnesium – important for photosynthesis – the plant's way of getting energy from the sun. Beware too much chicken manure can interfere with the availability of this essential nutrient.
* Sulphur – used by the plant to make chlorophyll, the thing that makes plants green.

TRACE ELEMENTS
* Boron – helps in the parts of the plant where they grow bigger like the shoots, flowers, and fruit.
* Iron & Manganese – used by the plant to make chlorophyll.
* Copper & zinc – are important in assisting with the tissue development in the plant.
* Molybdenum – helps the plant convert nitrogen into plant proteins.

Once again everyone's soil is different so some may be rich in nutrients while others may be poor.

SO WHAT EXACTLY ARE SOME OF THE THINGS YOU CAN ADD TO YOUR SOIL TO MAKE IT BETTER?

There are so many different ways to add goodness to your soil. We'll just look at the basics ones and when you get the hang of gardening next season you can explore the exciting world of compost teas and worm wees.

There are many ways to feed your plants.

Compost

The most common addition to the garden and can be easily obtained from garden centres at a reasonable price – however in some situations you get what you pay for. Even better – it is not difficult to make at home. Basically it is a combination of 1 part green, nitrogen-rich garden, waste (fresh lawn clippings and vegetable peelings) and 2 parts brown, carbon rich, dry waste (hay, shredded newspaper and cardboard) and it all rots down to give you a great soil conditioner.

Manure

The full set of NPK and trace elements can be found in all animal manures but you need to use more as they are in lower numbers. They also contain beneficial bacteria that is great for your plants and soil.

Vegetarian animal manure is preferable. Each farmyard animal brings its own value to the garden in its own special way.

- ✳ **Horses** – fantastic manure, but it needs to be left for six months to rot down a bit or it may be too strong for young plants.
- ✳ **Chickens** – also very good for the garden and also quite strong. The best way to use it would be to add it to the compost heap.

Planting a 'test plant' can show you what the soil is lacking. Plants almost have their own language to tell you what they need. The leaves can go yellow, brown, and purple, go splotchy or make their veins stand out or fade away. These are all ways the plant is telling you what it needs. Not all strange leaf behaviour is disease, so if your plants aren't doing well, have a search for leaves online – your plant may just be hungry.

Chicken manure is very good for the garden.

* **Sheep** – A nice mild additive and is readily available in pellet form in most garden centres.
* **Cows** – this is the best farmyard poop about. It isn't as strong as horse manure and breaks down in to a lovely soil conditioner packed full of great nutrients.

Word of caution: *Some weed killer residues can go straight through the animal and into the garden causing deformities in plants rendering the garden useless for many a season. If you can, ask if the farmer if it has been sprayed with a broadleaf herbicide. If the answer is yes, I would err on the side of caution and avoid it – as it is not worth ruining your garden over a bag of free manure on the side of a country lane.*

Blood and bone
This is dried and ground blood and bone and sometimes you can even find it with

TAKE NOTE
WHAT IS GOING ON IN YOUR
GARDEN THIS WEEK?

If you can, use a soil test kit to determine the NPK ratios in your garden.
What kind of amendments are you adding to your soil?

....

....

....

....

....

....

fish in it. It releases the nutrients slowly and is a good all round, organic rich fertiliser.

General fertiliser

An inorganic blend of chemicals created to meet the needs of the average garden. They have exactly known nutrient values. Follow the directions carefully to avoid damaging your plants as they can be quite concentrated. Too much fertiliser is a difficult problem to fix.

Other things you can add to your soil to give it a lift include, but is not limited to, mushroom compost, seaweed, leaf mould, comfrey and a subtle use of wood ash. There are so many options out there to cultivate the ideal soil for growing vegetables.

SAFETY FIRST: *it is important to wash your hands thoroughly after using soil amendments and most definitely before eating.*

SMALL SPACES? NO PROBLEM

As cities become more intensive, digging up the backyard is not an option for many

Allotment gardening Photo credit: Sean James Cameron at thehorticulturalchannel.com

Container gardening.

environment completely dependent on you for everything. The container itself needs to be as large as you can afford to buy and at least 40cm deep for growing vegetables. If you don't mind a 'shabby chic' look that is affordable, then popping some holes in the bottom of a bucket will give you a good size pot for most vegetable plants. These days they come in a lovely range of colours.

Normal garden dirt is not good for containers as it is too heavy and will compact and make it really hard work for any plants trying to grow in it. You need specialist container potting mix and once again you get what you pay for. Compost is also a welcome addition to any container.

It is even more important that you water and add nutrients regularly – maybe set up a schedule, as the need for free draining soil can often mean your plant food can escape easily. The good news is this kind of soil comes weed free; however, it won't stay like that so keep your eyes peeled as you don't want to lose precious food to interlopers.

as it is too small, rented or non-existent. However, this need not be a barrier to growing your own food. As demand grows so does innovation and there are many options available for those lacking in space. Vertical gardening is a fabulous way to grow crops on a balcony or up a sunny fence. There is a solution for most urban situations.

Looking beyond your boundaries can be a great way to grow food. Consider sharing space with a neighbour, join a community garden or sign up for an allotment in your local area.

Growing in Containers
This is quite different from gardening in the open ground. You are creating an

Harvesting of crops and removing the plants at the end of the season depletes your soil of goodness. Continually adding nutrients back in will keep a soil healthy. Not putting anything back into the soil is a great way to end up with a garden no good for growing anything.

Dig in good quality compost.

Filling raised beds

The soil within a raised bed will eventually become an extension of the existing soil, only above ground. Both will benefit from what they can offer each other like worms, bacteria and fungi moving into the raised bed and the compost, organic matter and nutrients migrating down.

Make sure you get the best soil you can afford. Answering an advert in the back of the local newspaper for free topsoil may seem like a bargain, however if the quality is poor or it is full of building rubble you are wasting your time and efforts. Having said that there are bargains to be had. Reputable suppliers should provide you with a quality soil with no hidden problems, however the quality will be reflected in the price.

Ask for a sample first and do all the tests to see what kind of soil it is. Also check it out for weeds. The last thing you want to do is bring in a nightmare.

EARLY SPRING

The most anticipated month of the whole calendar for the keen gardener. Finally, winter has been overthrown and spring is now upon us with its daffodils and tulips, baby lambs and the hope of an entire season resting on its fragile shoulders. But be warned, spring is a tumultuous season with the most unreliable weather of all the seasons. One moment it seems like the heady warm days are with us and it doesn't seem possible that it could change anytime soon. The next moment we are thrust back into the freezing cold gloom of winter and any gains made in the garden can quickly be lost. Spring is not your friend – Don't trust it!

Sow	*Plant*	*Maintain*	*Harvest*
• Outdoors – carrot, spinach, spring onion, parsnip, peas, radish and silverbeet.	• Plant seedlings of lettuce, leek, cabbage, broccoli, onion and silverbeet into the garden.	• Dig in generous amounts of compost and enrich soil before planting.	• Asparagus, beetroot, broadbean, cabbage, carrot, leek, lettuce, spring onion, parsnip, peas, radish, silverbeet and spinach.
• Indoors – beans, beetroot, broccoli, brussels sprouts, cabbage, cauliflower, celery, cucumber, eggplant, leek, lettuce, melon, pepper, pumpkin, squash, sweetcorn, tomato and zucchini/courgette.	• Plant asparagus crowns. • Plant onion sets. • Plant potatoes after chitting.	• Make sure greenhouses are well secured and have good airflow on hot days. • Construct sturdy frames and structures to support vegetables. • Install irrigation and test it works.	NOTE: This is just a guide – things may happen faster or slower in your garden.

Daffodils herald the start of the growing season

GETTING STARTED

Sowing seeds for a fabulous season

Surprisingly enough there is a lot of advice out there on how to get the best out of sowing seeds. It can seem daunting, but it is actually quite simple. The bonus is it is so much more affordable than seedlings, a lot more rewarding and will give you something to do as you wait for the weather to be warm enough to actually plant things in the garden.

The best advice is: Don't start too early!

In your enthusiasm to get going it can be tempting to start everything at once as soon as you can. This isn't such a good idea as each plant has different requirements to getting started. Peppers like a long head start in a warm spot however pumpkins only really need four weeks to get going before they out grow their pots and start flowering on your windowsill. Time spent finding how long your plants need between sowing and planting out will make all the difference to the long term health of your plants.

Sow seeds in alphabetical order and take a photo of the seed tray in case anything untoward happens to your labels.

When to start your tender seeds indoors:

Three Months before the last frost
* Eggplant
* Pepper
* Celery

Two Months before the last frost
* Tomato
* Sweetcorn
* Beans
* Melons

One Month before the last frost
* Lettuce
* Beans
* Pumpkin
* Squash
* Cucumber
* Zucchini

The seed packet may say it can be sown from early spring, but it may not be the case in your area. If you sow seeds too soon, then you will be left with large seedlings desperate to go out into the garden well before the conditions are suitable outside. Most seedlings need about six weeks to go from seed to being a good size to plant outside in the garden. Find out when your average last frost date is in your area count back start your seeds then.

Gather together everything you need.

What you need

❋ **Containers** – All you need is a suitable container with holes in the bottom for essential drainage. They can be purchased specifically for the task or upcycled from your recycling bin. Just make sure your containers are very clean. Hygiene is actually really important. They don't need to be very deep – about 5cm is a good depth for most seedlings.

❋ **Soil** – Seeds don't need a full nutrient rich soil. Everything they need to get started is already in the seed, like a packed lunch. If the soil is too rich it can harm the fragile seedling so it is best to start with a low nutrient soil blend.

I would recommend a specialist 'seed raising mix' to grow your seeds in as it has no nasty germs in it and is made of exactly the right mix of ingredients that will help your seeds germinate successfully. Some even contain a mild fungicide to prevent premature death of your seedlings. It has the perfect texture and is light and free from large lumps so the seedling can break through to the surface easily. There are many other options out there to try and you may experience successful germination but soil straight from the garden is not suitable for indoor sowing and I don't recommend it at all.

❋ **Labels** – Importantly don't forget to label your seeds. It is easy to think you will remember – but you never do. Make sure your label remains easy to read throughout the season without fading. This become especially important when you want to know the difference between mild pepper and a fiery chilli.

How to sow seeds

1. Fill your container with moist seed raising soil and gently firm down.
2. Sow your seeds. Lightly scatter seeds on the soil, pop one or two seeds in a hole or sprinkle thinly in a row.
3. Cover the seeds with seed raising soil to the right depth. Check the seed packet for exact instructions. The rule of thumb is as deep as three times the height of the seed.
4. Firm gently to make sure the seed has good contact with the damp soil so it can begin to grow.

A great season starts with one seed.

Make sure seeds are given enough space.

5. Put the container in a warm place and wait for the seedlings to emerge. Most seeds should sprout within 14 days, although some may take longer.

Watering – Keep the soil moist. Not too wet and not too dry. A spray bottle is really useful here and should be used little and often. If it gets too wet your seedlings may die.

Don't overdo it.
Space out the seeds well as crowded seedlings will have reduced airflow around them and are at risk of dying. Think about how many plants you will end up with when you just liberally sprinkle the seeds on. A packet of lettuce seeds can have up to 1000 and I'm pretty sure you don't need that many in your garden, coming ready all at the same time.

You don't need to sow too many more than you need. Double what you want to grow is about right, and have a spare set of seeds on standby – just in case of non-germination or tragic accident. Once all

Pop a mirror behind your seedlings on the window sill to reflect the light from the window back at the seedlings from the other side to prevent them leaning off towards the light. A plain flat mirror is best.

danger of frost has passed and everything you need is growing well, then you can give your spare seedlings away to friends and family.

Watch out for **Damping off**. *This is a disease that kills small seedlings in overcrowded situations with poor airflow, or it is too wet or cold.*

Light – When the seedlings emerge put them in a warm, sunny spot and continue to keep the soil damp. Seedlings without enough light will go all yellow, leggy (long and thin and weak) and will essentially be no good. Leggy plants often struggle and are never really healthy.

On a windowsill, turn the pots every day so they don't lean off in one direction as they grow towards the light.

Even better would be to pop them in a greenhouse or cold frame. These can range in value from a solid glass and aluminium structure, through to an affordable plastic covered frame. These mini greenhouses are really useful and do the job and are a great addition to your garden.

However, I would offer a word of caution: Make sure it is well anchored down. Weigh it down, tie it to something solid or screw it to a fence because with even the slightest gust of wind these things can fly off with your seedlings and this can be quite upsetting.

Paper and cardboard pots are good alternative containers but they can 'wick' the water away from the soil. The container itself pulls the moisture from the soil and your seeds won't germinate if it is too dry. Keep the soil moist but don't be tempted to over water or your seeds will rot.

Make sure the seeds have good contact with the soil and water lightly.

Protection

Seeds planted outdoors are vulnerable to a number of pests. You need to protect your emerging seedlings from slugs, snails, cats and birds. There are many solutions out there, and you need to find the one that works best for you in your garden.

Sowing outdoors

Not all plants like being started in pots indoors. Some don't mind it, but prefer to be planted directly into the soil. This commonly applies to carrots, parsnips and other root crops and can affect the way they grow. Check on the seed packet as these aren't the only ones.

Sowing seeds out in the open is quite easy. Make sure the soil is warm enough. Seeds will rot away in cold, wet soil and you will have wasted your efforts. There is an old wives' tale that suggests that back in the day garden apprentices would whip down their trousers and sit on the soil. If they could finish their lunch comfortably then the soil was good to go. Generally, the temperature you are looking for is about 15°C but warmer is better. Look into what your seeds prefer.

Focus on your spacing, don't sow them too deep. Peas, beans and sweetcorn can be laid on the soil so you can see the spacing and then gently push the seed into the soil with your fore finger to a depth of your first knuckle and then gently pull the soil over the top.

TAKE NOTE
WHAT IS GOING ON IN YOUR GARDEN THIS WEEK?

Which seeds are you sowing now? Which will you leave until later? Note down if they are indoor or outdoor seeds.

Record the seeds you have sown. You can find a grid at the back of the book on page 218.

RECORD KEEPING

Record keeping –
remembering for next year

Sometimes remembering what you did a year ago can a bit of a hazy memory so taking notes and writing things down can be very helpful, not just for looking back but for looking forward.

This information is more useful than just knowing what you are growing this season, but using it to make long term use of what you are doing for the benefit of the seasons to come. Over time you can develop an extensive guide for what works best in your garden, your specific weather patterns, the things you like to eat and what grows easily for you.

Using your computer can be quite useful for keeping notes as it can become searchable and if you want to know when you started your tomato seeds last year then it is at your fingertips!

Write it all down

When you plant your seeds in the ground, write it down in here, on a calendar or in a notebook. Every time you notice something or do something with that plant then make a note – the date and what you did.

Mark in your calendar the number of days expected to have a harvest from planting out your seedlings or seeds, so you know when to go and look for the ripe fruit. With some it is quite obvious – if a tomato is red, eat it! But for some of the more hidden ones like carrots, potatoes and sweetcorn, a rough estimate of when to harvest is handy to know so you don't dig them up too early and be disappointed, or go too late and find them past their best.

Write down what the quality and the flavour of the vegetables was like when you harvest them so next year you will know to wait a bit longer or get in earlier. Only experience in your garden will help you refine this over time.

Take lots of photos of your garden.

Label seeds well.

Keep a close eye on what the weather does.

at these are as learning opportunities so you are not doomed to have failure next time you encounter an old foe of a weather pattern.

Gardens constantly provide learning opportunities and even the most expert seasoned gardener will willingly admit they don't know everything. But the most important thing is to learn how your garden grows, and time and experience will give you that.

Make a folder in your computer called 'veggie garden' and have a folder within it for the year and then folders for the months and so you can see how big things grow and what they look like while they are growing. Re-familiarise yourself with this at the beginning of each season to help you with your spacing, or support structures and so you can make modifications to your techniques going forward.

The weather

Record unusual weather events so you can learn what happens in your garden, as each garden has specific microclimates created by hills, fences, trees, drainage and altitude. Record frosts so you know when the first and last one typically is. Note down terrible storms so you begin to appreciate that early spring is a hostile time in the garden.

If the summer turns out to be a drought, then write down what you did to cope with it and how well it worked so you will remember next time you encounter a drought, or a wet summer or a windy one. Each summer will present a different set of circumstances and they best way to look

TAKE NOTE

WHAT IS GOING ON IN YOUR
GARDEN THIS WEEK?

Are you still digging in the garden to get it ready? Have any seeds germinated this week? Are you still getting frosts?

WAITING... WAITING... WAITING...

Avoid the urge to poke.

This can be a frustrating time for the keen gardener. The plans have been made and the garden dug over and ready and waiting and depending on your location you will now find yourself at varying stages of the seed sowing process. But mostly you will be at that stage where it seems like you have been waiting an eternity and there isn't even a hint of green.

Avoid all temptation to poke about in the seed trays – they will come up, so long as you have kept the soil warm and moist but not wet or dry! However, if you don't see signs of life after two weeks it may be a good idea to sow your spare seeds.

What you can do this week is go out into the garden and check for weeds. All the digging you have done will have disturbed weed seeds and with the slowly warming season there will be stirrings of life. At this stage a gentle hoe or rake across the top of the soil will be enough to disturb the tiny weed roots and will keep the garden weed-free.

POTATOES

If the thought of a lovely new potato freshly plucked from the soil and slathered in butter seems like a great idea, now is a good time to consider growing some for a summer harvest.

How to Grow

It is best to start from seed potatoes from a reputable supplier to ensure they are free from disease. Deciding which potato to grow from the many varieties available depends on how you want to eat them.

Chitting

You can help your potatoes get started by putting your seed potatoes in a dry place with good airflow, out of direct sunlight and little shoots will begin to sprout. This does help, but isn't necessary and you can plant them straight away.

You can also plant them in containers – two or three spuds in each one. Start with the container a third deep and plant your potatoes in that. As they grow gradually fill the container with more soil.

Growing

Gently plant each potato about 10cm deep and 25cm apart. It may seem strange but as the potato grows bury the leaves and mound up the soil until you have a pile about 30cm high. This is especially important in the early days as it will help protect them from any frosts. This also prevents potatoes from being exposed to the sun and turning green.

Harvesting

Depending on the variety you have grown, the potatoes will be ready to harvest after between 90 to 150 days in the ground. (Check the seed potato packet for details). However, the plants themselves can give you a few clues on when to harvest.

✳ For nice fresh new potatoes, you can dig them up from when they begin to flower.

✳ With some of the early varieties that don't need as long in the ground it is best to harvest them when the flowers begin to die down. (Although there are some varieties that don't flower so use your calendar as well.)

✳ You can eat the spuds at any stage from those first stolen ones, but the longer you leave them the bigger they will be.

✳ With the late varieties, they are ready to harvest when the plants die down and are all brown and shrivelled.

To keep the soil moist try resting your seed trays and pots on top of wet newspaper and keep the newspaper wet so the soil sucks up the moisture it needs.

Make sure you dig up every last one or next year you will have potatoes popping up among your peas!

TAKE NOTE
WHAT IS GOING ON IN YOUR GARDEN THIS WEEK?

Have any seedlings popped up? How long did it take? How cold has it been overnight?

Bury your chitted potatoes deep.

Mound up the soil as the plant grows.

Bandicooting is when you ever so gently rummage around in the soil under the plant until you find enough spuds for your dinner, and then cover it all back up, trying not to damage anything so the rest of the potatoes can carry on growing big and fat.

A word of caution – don't eat the berries that form after the flowers on the top of the plant – they are very poisonous and it is best to pick them off as they are stealing energy from the potatoes underground.

Also don't eat any green potatoes. These have been exposed to the sun and this causes them to become toxic.

Storage

Store the potatoes in a cool, dark place, in a cardboard box, paper bag or hessian sack. New potatoes won't store well.

Take care when digging up the potatoes.

TRANSPLANTING

When seedlings first appear from the soil they have a set of leaves that often look nothing like the leaves on the adult plant. These are called the seed leaves and contain the nutrients the plant needs to get going. The next set of leaves look more like what they are supposed to and are called the true leaves. These are normal fully functioning leaves that create energy for the plant from the process called photosynthesis. Once the first set of true leaves are big and strong it is time to transplant the seedling from the seed raising soil with minimal nutrients, to a more nutritious mix.

With transplanting, you need to just gradually move the plant into ever so slightly bigger pots until it is time to move it into the garden. This helps the plant to develop a strong root ball. If you just put it in a large pot straight away, the roots will end up weak and leggy.

Seedlings need to be transplanted frequently as they grow or the plant will become root bound. The roots can be damaged or suffocated, which results in slowed growth and the plant doesn't look very healthy.

It isn't recommended to do this in the heat of the day as it stresses the plant out too much.

✳ The container – Once again it doesn't really matter what you use, as long as it is clean and has good drainage.

For the first transplant you should start with a pot about 5cm across and then eventually moving up to pots about 10cm or even 15cm before going into the garden.

✳ The soil – So you don't shock your plants, gradually increase the richness of the soil. A 50:50 mix of potting mix and compost, with a dash of blood and bone is a great start. Then use compost and soil from your lovingly prepared gardens at a 50:50 mix and eventually just use the soil from the garden, however I would avoid garden soil for the tiniest seedlings to reduce the risk of disease. If you think about it, it is a little like weaning a baby onto grown up food.

The process

Give the plant a good watering and allow the soil to drain. A seaweed tonic is great to avoid transplant shock and settle them in nicely, but isn't essential.

If it is in a pot by itself, put your hand across the top of the pot with the plant stem between your fingers and turn the pot upside down. Give it a tap and the plant should pop out, then gently hold it by the root ball.

If your seedlings are in a seed container with other plants in individual cells, give the bottom of the pot a bit of a squeeze to loosen the root ball. Poking a pencil through the drainage holes can help the root ball to rise out of the pot.

IT IS IMPORTANT NOT TO HOLD ONTO, OR PUT PRESSURE ON THE STEM. This can cause damage and affect the way the plant grows and also invite disease into the bruised part. Also be very careful of the growing tip as to damage this will stop the plant growing upwards. You can gently hold a plant by the leaves as they aren't as important to the forming structure of the plant and if it gets damaged then just pinch the leaf off. The plant will recover.

If the seedlings are in an open tray where they are all in together – get a plant label or a pencil and gently poke the tip into the soil, hold the seedling by a leaf and gently lever the seeding from the soil to free the roots.

If the root ball looks root bound, then gently tease them to stop the roots going around in circles.

Most plants need to be planted at the same level they were in the previous pot – which would be the same level that they were when they came up as seeds.

Before you take the seedling out of the seed raising soil, fill the new pot to the point where the seedling roots would be resting on the soil.

❋ Remove the seedling and gently hold it in place in the new pot with one hand and with the other fill in the soil around the roots until it reaches the point where the soil was before.

❋ Firm the soil down gently and give it a tap to settle the soil around the roots.

❋ Give it another drink of water.

❋ Don't forget to pop in a label.

Roots coming out the bottom is a good indication it is time to transplant.

Root bound seedlings.

Tomatoes – are different from most of the other plants. They can be buried deep, and it is actually good for them, because they can grow roots out of the stem. This may seem strange but it gives the tomato a great start, a huge root structure and it is so deep that the plant won't have to worry too much about the top of the soil drying out as it will be able to find the moisture deep down in the garden.

TAKE NOTE

WHAT IS GOING ON IN YOUR GARDEN THIS WEEK?

Are any of your seedlings ready to transplant yet? Have you had a lot of rain? How much? Have you had to restart any seedlings?

....

....

....

....

Gently tease out the roots.

MID-SPRING

Normally in spring there is a really warm, sunny patch about halfway through and it can give an enthusiastic gardener a false sense of security. They plant out seedlings either lovingly cared for from a tiny seed or acquired with hard-earned cash, only to find the warm spell was an anomaly and winter-like weather returns to put the boot in once more as it leaves us for the last time. The problem is your tender seedlings can't cope with this and either perish or struggle to thrive and never catch up! This is a time to watch the weather carefully.

Sow

- Outdoors – beetroot, Brussels sprouts, cabbage, carrot, celery, leek, spinach, spring onion, parsnip, peas, radish and silverbeet.

- Indoors – beans, broccoli, cauliflower, celery, cucumber, eggplant, lettuce, melon, pepper, pumpkin, squash, sweetcorn, tomato and zucchini. (Can be sown into the garden if the soil is warm enough.)

- Succession sow – beetroot, broccoli, carrot, lettuce, radish, spring onion and sweetcorn every 3 weeks or so.

Plant

- Plant seedlings of beans, beetroot, broccoli, Brussels sprouts, cabbage, cauliflower, celery, cucumber, eggplant, leek, lettuce, melon, pepper, pumpkin, squash, sweetcorn, tomato and zucchini if the soil is warm enough.

- Plant asparagus crowns.

- Plant potatoes after chitting.

Maintain

- Dig in generous amounts of compost and enrich soil before planting.

- Make sure greenhouses are well secured and have good airflow on hot days.

- Construct sturdy frames and structures to support vegetables.

- Install irrigation and test it works.

Harvest

- Asparagus, beetroot, broadbean, cabbage, carrot, lettuce, peas, radish, spinach, spring onion, spinach and strawberries.

NOTE: This is just a guide – things may happen faster or slower in your garden.

A garden full of hope.

PATIENCE IS A VIRTUE

Wait until your last frost date before planting things into the garden. Although you still need to keep your wits about you and keep an eye on the weather as there is always a risk of frost for a few weeks beyond this date.

It is such a cliché but 'spring has sprung' and now more than ever you need to understand the third key to a good veggie garden and that is TIMING!

We will have had some warm sunny days by now and begun to get a sense of what summer will be like. We are all in a hurry for the warm weather to come and with that we can be tempted to start our veggie gardens too early. This is not a good idea.

Growing things from seed on windowsills and in greenhouses is a great way to keep your green thumbs from itching too much. Although not all things should be sown at the same time. Experience can teach you this, however it would be quicker if you learnt from my mistakes:

"*The importance of timing is something I have learnt the hard way and early one season I enthusiastically planted everything at once in my shiny new greenhouse. My greenhouse was large and I was keen to fill it – so fill it I did. I planted everything at the same time quite early in the spring. Everything grew well in the warmth of the greenhouse, however, the problem was my garden wasn't ready and neither was the weather.*

That year was a huge learning curve about the timings associated with seed sowing. Most of the plants grew too big and became entangled in the other plants and damage was done to the thug and the victim as I tried to free them. Cucumbers, pumpkins and peas are the worst offenders as they have tendrils that grab onto anything within a country mile.

The zucchinis were keen to get going and started flowering and producing fruit in their seed tray and I ended up harvesting the entire radish crop right there in the greenhouse!

Some out grew their pots and became root bound. This is a problem for most plants, but in particular brassicas as once they become root bound or dry in their pots they never recover properly and will struggle to do what they are supposed to in the big garden.

I had beans that were so long and leggy that they just flopped about the place once I planted them out they never really grew straight and tall. The sweetcorn seemed ok, but at the first breath of wind in the big garden the roots which hadn't been able to really settle in properly caused the plants to grow on an angle. This didn't bode well for the cobs as the pollen couldn't get to the kernels underneath and the whole crop had a strip of kernels on one side missing.

I found I hadn't planted the peppers and eggplants early enough and struggled to get a harvest at all."

I look back on that time and shudder. It was chaos and not my finest gardening

Don't trust the spring weather.

hour! Many of the plants struggled to catch up and my harvest wasn't as good as it could have been. Seed sowing is best done to suit the timings of the seed not the desires of the gardener.

Planting early handicaps your plants
It seems logical that if you plant things early then you will get an early harvest. Sadly, it doesn't work this way. Plants have their own special timing.

Plants will suffer if the soil is too cold or too damp and the light levels aren't yet strong enough as the days are still too short. And we don't need to mention the devastating effects of a late frost.

Seeds planted outside too early can rot in the soil, or just fail to germinate at all, when in a week or so the conditions would be ideal and germination comes easily.

Seedlings transplanted into these conditions can suffer in many different ways. Growth can be stunted, but not always. Broccoli for example can grow just fine with loads of strong leaves and you think you have gotten away with it, then the actual broccoli head doesn't form or it is so small it would be considered bite-sized. Or a plant will grow well but won't linger at the edible stage and race ahead and set seeds in the blink of an eye. All the plant is doing is taking up space and not earning its keep by giving you anything to eat!

These plants will be naturally weak and sickly and this will put them at risk from pests and diseases throughout the growing season. A hungry bug can spot a vulnerable plant from miles off and it won't have the energy to fend off any diseases that may come its way.

Plants transplanted too early very rarely produce a great crop. More often than not seedlings planted out at the correct time will overtake the early ones as they haven't had to struggle with the elements to get on with the business of growing. Spending the season problem-solving poorly plants isn't going to make for an enjoyable gardening experience.

So hold tight and wait and you will have a healthier crop to show for it!

TAKE NOTE
WHAT IS GOING ON IN YOUR GARDEN THIS WEEK?

How is the weather in your area? Is it normal for this time of year? How are your seedlings going?

....

....

....

....

HARDENING OFF

By now you should have some lovely healthy seedlings, however don't be tempted to plant them out – not yet. It may seem lovely and warm outside, but the thing is, it is not safe for the plants to go out yet.

They need to be prepared for the big wide world. They need to get used to the climate in your garden. It will be quite different from the cosy warmth of the greenhouse or window sill. If you just planted them straight out from indoors into the garden they won't like it. It is a harsh world out there. They could go into what is known as 'transplant shock' and slow or stop growing. They need to acclimatise. It could cause long-term damage that would result in stunted plants, a reduced harvest or in some cases death. Cucumbers can be particularly fussy if the weather isn't warm enough. You have to ease them into the real world, like a reluctant swimmer getting into a cold swimming pool… Slowly and gently.

Seedlings enjoy a day in the sun

The process

1. About a week or two before your last frost date, in the morning take all your plants and put them outside in a warm sunny spot out of the breeze and leave them there all day and then bring them in again at night.
2. Then the next day put them back outside and this time allow them to feel a gentle breeze through their leaves and put them away again at night.
3. Continue this each day for at least a week and ideally two weeks, gradually exposing them to the full extent of the weather they would experience in the garden.
4. Towards the end of this in and out routine, in a sheltered spot where they would be protected from any possible frost, leave them out overnight a couple of times.
5. Then come the date it is safe to plant them out, they will be completely acclimatised to life on the outside and will slip into the garden without even noticing too much that life has changed and will continue growing happily.
6. Watering them in with a seaweed solution can also help minimise the shock and help the roots to establish in the new location.
7. I can't say it enough: **Don't trust the weather**

Soil dried out by the wind can become so dry that it actually repels water and normal watering won't fix it. What you need to do is to immerse the whole plant in a bucket of water, some seaweed solution will help here too. Float the pot and allow it to sink to the bottom in its own time and then wait until the bubbles stop coming and then wait a little bit longer and then pull the plant out of the bucket and let it drain and you will find that the soil has rehydrated and you can carry on as normal.

TAKE NOTE
WHAT IS GOING ON IN YOUR
GARDEN THIS WEEK?

How warm is the soil getting? Which seedlings have begun the process of hardening off? Is the soil still weed free or have you had to rake it over again?

....

....

....

....

....

There is always a risk of a late frost so just to be safe – keep one eye on the overnight forecast and keep that frost cloth handy. This is also why we grow spare seedlings, in case of disaster.

Don't feel you have to plant your seedlings out on the last frost date. This is the 'first' date where it is deemed safe to plant things out – not the 'only' date. If your seedlings are too small – less than about 6cm or don't look strong enough, then leave them inside for another week or so. It won't harm them and in fact you are doing them a favour and they will get a better start to life on the outside.

Wind – a blessing and a curse

Plants exposed to a mild wind grow stronger and thicker than those in a sheltered position as their cell walls adapt to the conditions and make the plant more resilient. If you took a plant straight from the greenhouse or sunny window sill and planted it in the garden, not only will it be shocked by the temperature, but it would also be skinny and weak and not as prepared for life in the garden as a plant that had been hardened off properly.

Although take care as if the wind is too strong it can burn the leaves and dry out the soil. So you need to use your judgement. If it is too windy weather while hardening off your plants, then put them in a sheltered place or keep them tucked up in the greenhouse.

Quenching the thirst of dried pots

PLANTING OUT

If your seedlings are too small when they go out, then they won't be strong enough will struggle to thrive.

After months of preparation, it all comes down to this. The garden is good to go. The risk of frost has all but gone (although keep your eye firmly on the weather forecast for another couple of weeks yet), the weather is warming up and your plants by now should be used to life on the outside. There is nothing stopping you from finally planting out your garden, unless they are still too small.

❋ The tomatoes, peppers and broccoli should be around at least 10–15 cm tall.

❋ Zucchini and cucumbers should have at least two sets of true leaves and if you are in any doubt with these it is better to wait as they will really struggle if they find themselves outside when they aren't ready.

❋ Lettuce should have at least four leaves that are about 6cm longish.

❋ Beans should have two sets of true leaves. If they aren't there yet, they won't suffer from another week or so on the inside in fact they will thank you for it.

It always seems the strangest thing to take the seedlings you have tenderly nurtured and put them in the dirt and leave them there, but that is what needs to happen. There are a few simple steps to make the process easy on the plants and reduce the stress so that they can continue growing with minimal disruption.

The process:

1. Early in the morning of the day you will be planting out, give the plants a good drink of water or liquid feed to make sure they are strong and ready to go.

2. The best time for transplanting is in the late afternoon after the heat of the day or on a cloudy day when the sun isn't so strong. If you have to plant in the middle of the day, set up some shade for the plants until the heat of the sun has passed.

3. Dig the hole first, with the correct spacing from the other plants and in the nice rich soil you have prepared weeks ago.

4. Try not to yank the plants out of the pot by the stem as this can damage it for the rest of its life. Give the pot a bit of a squeeze and then with your fingers over the top of the pot turn it upside down and give it a tap and the seedling should pop out into your hand.

5. Be gentle with the roots, but give them a bit of a squeeze to loosen them and untangle any root-bound ones.

Settling into their new home.

All set to grow up.

6. It is important to plant the seedlings at the same soil level they were in the pot. Any deeper and the stem may rot. The exception to this is tomatoes as the deeper the better as they can grow roots out of the stem and make a stronger plant.

> *If you aren't sure your plants are big enough, go to a garden centre and have a look at the ones for sale there. These are the right size for planting out. But just look, don't buy any – you haven't got the room!*

7. Hold the seedling above the hole at the correct depth with one hand and with the other; fill the hole with soil, gently covering the roots.
8. Then give it a good drink of water. This helps the plant to overcome the shock and settles the soil around the roots.
9. Now is a good time to put in any support structures, stakes and irrigation systems as it could damage the plant to install them retrospectively.

10. Don't forget to label your plants and protect them from slugs and snails.
11. The plants may look droopy for a couple of days – but make sure the soil doesn't dry out and they should bounce back in a no time.

SAVING THE SPRING SHOWERS

One thing you may want to look into for the season ahead: WATER.

Unfortunately not everyone will have free access to their own water. If you are going to have to rely on your tap, then in this crazy world it could end up costing you, as gardens can be quite thirsty places.

Now is a good time to start thinking about collecting rainwater from the lovely spring showers, so you won't have to rely so heavily on the tap. If you have a look online there are lots of helpful, homemade and realistic ideas that will suit your situation so you can start saving now for a wetter future!

TAKE NOTE
WHAT IS GOING ON IN YOUR GARDEN THIS WEEK?

Have you followed the plan when planting plants in the garden? How can you save water?

Take photos, it will surprise you in a week or two how quickly they have grown.

....

....

....

PEST WATCH

The challenge with sowing seeds and transplanting seedlings outside is they need protecting from bad things. Bad things like cats using your garden as a litter box, birds scratching up your seeds for a tasty treat and slugs and snails eating the seedling the minute it shows itself above the soil. It is quite frustrating to look out over your garden the day after you lovingly planted everything out to find most of your seedlings have completely vanished without a trace.

Keeping a close eye on what is going on in and around your garden will help you to stay on top of potential problems. It is always better to be proactive than reactive when it comes to pests.

Cats

These have to be the most annoying pests as their contribution to disaster is twofold. Firstly, they see the freshly tilled soil as an ideal place to use as a litter box and scratch about the place making the perfect spot for themselves. They have no regard for the carefully sown seeds in perfect rows or the barely visible emerging seedlings. Thanks to the neighbourhood cats an orderly garden with neat rows can end up with the jumbled style of a cottage garden.

A more serious problem is the deposit they leave behind and stumbling across one unwittingly and barehanded can be a nasty surprise. It can also a huge risk of disease and illness, especially if you are gardening with young children. If you do encounter a cat contribution, just remove the offending mess and wash your spade and hands thoroughly. The soil in the garden will still be perfectly fine to grow vegetables in.

The best solution is to prevent the cats in the first place and a physical barrier is the easiest.

Loads of plastic forks or bamboo kebab skewers poked into your garden with the pointy end up around your seeds and seedlings will give kitty nowhere to sit!

✳ Holly, rose bush prunings and other prickly plants laid over the soil will make it most uncomfortable for use as a loo.

✳ But a much simpler way is to put down

TAKE NOTE
WHAT IS GOING ON IN YOUR GARDEN THIS WEEK?

Which pests are causing you the greatest problems? How have you dealt with them and what kind of success have you had?

....

....

....

....

....

....

....

Opposite: Cats can be a huge threat to a young garden.

Protect your seedlings from cats.

a plastic trellis or some netting over your soil and lift it off once your plants are strong enough for cats to see there is actually something growing there.

This is a temporary problem, until the garden fills in, but it is an annoying one to have.

Birds

The start of the growing season also coincides with nesting season and the garden becomes filled with busy birds looking, not only to feed themselves, but nestfuls of hungry chicks. Your garden becomes like a supermarket for them with a wide variety of options. They will scratch about and dig up your worms, steal your seeds, peck at your first red strawberry and even have the audacity to nibble the leaves of your tender seedlings.

The only real way to stop the birds is to throw a net over everything you want to protect. Although it needs to be well covered as they will find a way in and in some cases may not find a way out. Take care to arrange your netting in a way that the birds don't become entangled in it.

Slugs and snails

These are the worst. They are mostly nocturnal and slime their way all over your garden chomping their way through your tender seedlings. They can decimate a garden overnight leaving just a slime trail to show for their efforts. They spend the day hiding away in dark places.

You can tackle them in many ways:

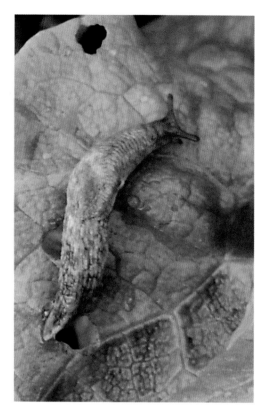

This can demolish your seedlings overnight.

* Collection – You can take a torch and go hunting at night. You will soon have a bucketful of them, but unless you have chickens you still have a problem. Lobbing them over the fence isn't an option as they will make their way back home.

* Traps – Creating a cosy dark place like under a strategically placed board, up-turned flower pot or other container can provide somewhere for them to retreat to after a hard night marauding in your garden. Each morning you can collect them and move them far away.

* Sharp objects, and scratchy surfaces and things they don't like such as eggshells

Snail eggs

and coffee grinds are said to be a deterrent, however they aren't reliable and not worth risking your tending seedlings with.

✳ Beer traps – are great. Bury a container with steep sides – like a margarine container into the garden and fill with beer. They can't help themselves and are drawn to the liquor in great numbers. The biggest problem with this method is you have to empty it regularly and the stink is quite vile.

✳ Copper tape – gives them a little electric shock and they don't like to cross it. However, it needs to be a good width – at least 5cm in a continuous strip around the area you want to protect. It also needs to stay shiny as it loses its effect when it tarnishes. It is good for pots and small areas, but quite costly and impractical for a whole garden.

✳ Bait – this is a tried and true method – they love to eat it and it kills them

before they get to your plant. However, there are risks associated. You don't really want the birds eating the carcasses. Making covered slug feeding stations will keep the dead and dying out of sight and out of reach. It can be harmful to pets so please keep these products out of reach of your dogs. Follow the directions on the packet and with sensible use everyone, including your plants will stay safe.

The choice is yours as to how you protect your seedlings here, however a proven remedy is often best here. A slug or snail can devastate your entire crop in one evening and it is heartbreaking and even more so to lose your crop in spite of your best efforts.

Other pests will make their way into your garden over the season, however for now these are the ones you need to watch out for.

LATE SPRING

By and large the cold weather is behind you now and you can feel the promise of summer in the air. The garden should start to have that established feel about it as tender seedlings begin to bulk out and take their place. Weeding and watering become everyday tasks and are often a great way to unwind at the end of a busy day. For the gardener, after months of hard work to get the garden to this point, late spring is a time to relax a little and watch the plants grow as you wait for the harvest. Take the time to feel proud of all you have achieved so far.

Sow

- Outdoors – beetroot, broccoli, Brussels sprouts, cabbage, cauliflower, carrot, celery, leek, lettuce, spinach, spring onion, parsnip, radish and silverbeet.

- Indoors – beans, cucumber, eggplant, melon, pepper, pumpkin, squash, sweetcorn, tomato and zucchini. (Can be sown into the garden if the soil is warm enough.)

- Succession sow – beetroot, broccoli, carrot, lettuce, radish, spinach, spring onion and sweetcorn every three weeks or so.

Plant

- Plant seedlings of beans, broccoli, cauliflower, celery, cucumber, eggplant, lettuce, melon, pepper, pumpkin, squash, sweetcorn, tomato and zucchini if the soil is warm enough.

- Plant potatoes after chitting.

Maintain

- Regular deep watering is best.

- Remove laterals from tomatoes.

- Remove weeds while they are small.

- Feed plants weekly or fortnightly with a liquid feed.

- Keep an eye out for pests and disease – be prepared to act quickly!

Harvest

- Asparagus, beetroot, broadbean, cabbage, carrot, garlic, lettuce, onion, peas, potato, radish, shallots, silverbeet, spinach, spring onion, strawberries and zucchini.

NOTE: This is just a guide – things may happen faster or slower in your garden..

Spinach flourishing in the late spring sun.

WATERING

Now your plants are in the garden, you can relax a little, however, there are still things that need to be done. You need to remove any weed that dares raise its ugly head in your lovely garden – while it is little! You need to take up a daily pest control check and make sure there are no nasty bugs wreaking havoc in your patch, and deal with them as soon as you see them.

But the most important thing to be taking care of is watering! Gardens can be thirsty places. Firstly while working hard in the garden, you will probably work up a bit of a sweat! Stay hydrated and drink lots of water so you stay healthy enough to tend to your plants, especially as the weather warms up into summer.

But the really thirsty creatures of the garden are plants, and without enough water they will struggle to thrive and your harvest will be compromised. Pests and disease can spot a thirsty, stressed plant a mile off. So you really need to think about your options now, before you find yourself in the middle of a drought.

HOW THE PLANTS LIKE TO RECEIVE THEIR WATER

Hate getting their leaves wet
✳ Water at the roots

cucumber	potatoes	tomato
peas	pumpkin	zucchini

Overhead irrigation.

Don't mind getting their leaves wet

❇ Safe to use overhead watering

beans	eggplant	radish
brassicas	garlic	salad
beetroot	onions	silverbeet
carrot	parsnip	spinach
sweetcorn	pepper	turnips / swedes

Watering first thing in the morning is the best time, before the heat of the day, so the moisture has a good chance to sink in. Midday isn't really suitable as the evaporation is strong and there is the possibility of droplets magnifying the sunlight and burning your leaves.

Evening is better than midday, but the damp environment tends to linger longer without the heat of the day and can create ideal conditions for disease. But you can only do what you can do – so keep a close eye on your moisture levels and the health of your plants.

Make sure you water consistently – set up a routine. A deep watering every other day is much better than a short splash every day. A short splash will cause the roots to grow near the surface as that is where they expect to find the water. This makes them susceptible to drying out on a breezy day or if you miss a day watering. So on the whole you will have weaker plants.

A good long soak every other day will mean the roots will go down deep looking for the water and will make the plant stronger and healthier. They won't rely entirely on you for their moisture, as enough should be stored deep down in the soil. Missing a day here and

If you do have plants in the ground and the weather makes an unexpected turn back to icy conditions, you can make a mini cloche by cutting the bottom out of a large, clear plastic container.

Water deeply with a hose.

Soaker hose delivers water to the roots.

TAKE NOTE
WHAT IS GOING ON IN YOUR GARDEN THIS WEEK?

When was the last time you had rain? How much did you get? What is the coldest overnight temperature? How hot is it getting during the day? What have you planted out this week? Have you noticed any pests?

there wouldn't be as much of a problem. But use your common sense – if the plant is wilting, give it a drink. If the ground is wet – don't!

FROST

Depending on where you live will determine what you are up to in the garden. During this time of year in late spring much of what goes on is dictated by the weather and even those in sunny places may still find themselves at the mercy of a late frost. The greatest guide to the gardener is the weather forecast. But also common sense. If it is one of those clear evenings with a touch of chill to it, don't take the risk, spread frost cloth across your tender seedlings.

Temperatures may fall into the icy range in your garden or in certain spots while your neighbour may not get a frost at all. Cold air is heavier than warm air and can settle in low lying or sheltered parts of the garden. It really pays to know your garden. Where a frost is likely to linger, avoid

planting tender seedlings in those spots or wait until the risk of frost is past.

If your ground is still a little too cold or the risk of frost is too much, don't be tempted to plant things out, your time will come soon enough. The first frost-free date is generally the average first date, but by no means the only date and you generally have a month or two to get things planted out safely. If in doubt – wait.

Potato tip
Once your potatoes begin to emerge from the soil, grab a hoe and cover them back up to create a mound around them. This not only provides a protection from late frosts, but will extend the underground stem the potatoes grow from and will increase your yield.

MULCH

Bare soil is not a natural state in nature and so weeds will always try and colonise it. Also the soil doesn't react too well to being bare in the hot summer months. It can form a crust that will actually repel water, so you can water as much as you like, but it won't soak into the root zone where it is needed most. Mulch can be a great way to keep the moisture in the soil and the weeds down around your plants so it is win-win!

But not all mulches are created equally.

Never put mulch up and around the base of plants it can reduce airflow and rot the stem.

Wood chips

As the wood breaks down, large wood chips can actually draw the nutrients from the soil that your plants need to grow. So it can be counter-productive. They will also cause problems getting a fine tilth (soft fluffy soil with hardly any lumps) for sowing seeds directly into the garden next season as wood generally takes 3–5 years to break down. Once it has broken down it is a rich fertile mix, but until then it is a lumpy, nutrient thief that is difficult to work around.

Sawdust

This can also work well as it would be quicker to break down than bark chips – although it can be a little acidic and will still rob the soil of nutrients – so feed well with blood and bone and maybe add regular doses of lime. Also check it comes from untreated wood.

Pea straw

A thick layer of this is a good choice as it breaks down over the season and not only keeps the moisture in and weeds down, but as it breaks down it gives goodness back to the soil.

The down side is the bales may have pea seeds in it that will germinate and grow. Although the roots will fix nitrogen and enrich the soil, they could attract mildew into the garden – so it is best just to pull them out.

Compost

Some places recommend compost as a good mulch, although I can't quite understand this. Yes, a good layer of compost will keep the moisture in, but it is also a rich, fertile growing medium – perfect for weeds to grown on top of! So I'm not convinced about this one.

Weed matting

While this may seem like a simple easy solution, it can actually damage the soil and make it 'sour' (a little too acid).

Rain is unable to penetrate through the weed matting efficiently. Airflow is restricted and the sun heats up the ground below it as most of the matting you will find is black and so it can do a bit of damage to you soil ecosystem. Slugs tend to like hiding in its folds and the most determined weeds find a way through but become stuck tight so it makes it really hard to remove. They arc also made from non-biodegradable plastic so aren't all that environmentally friendly.

Lawn clippings

These may seem like a good free idea, however there are a few drawbacks. Fresh grass clippings are full of nitrogen, and in most cases you don't want to encourage a fast green growth that is all lush but has no substance. You need a slow, steady balanced growth. Also grass clippings have a tendency to go mushy and rot and stink, but also exclude the air from the soil, turning it sour and harming your plants. It can also introduce weed seeds that may be growing in your lawn. However, if you allow your grass clippings to dry out and apply them, gradually in light fluffy layers you should get away with it – just keep an eye out for weeds.

Hay

May seem like a good cheap idea, but hay is *full* of weed and grass seeds and you might as well chuck lawn seed over your garden and be done with it!

Mulch can bring great benefit to the garden.

Straw

This is good to use, but not all that easy to get hold of. If you can get your hands on some then go for it.

Newspaper

This is a great way to upcycle and help out your garden. Shredded is better than whole sheets, but it should be kept damp or it will blow away! Try not to use the shiny printed paper as the ink isn't as friendly. If you are concerned about the ink, give your local newspaper office a call and ask. The downside here, apart from it wanting to blow away, is it does look a little ugly.

Leaves

Collected last autumn and shredded, leaves are a perfect mulch – you just need to have a very big tree to get enough leaves… or sneak out to parks in the middle of the night and grab some!

THINNING

As seeds sown directly into the soil begin to appear, now is a good time to thin them out, while they are still small and won't disturb the roots of their neighbours. This means checking the seed packet to see how far apart they should be and then removing seedlings evenly along the row to make sure plants don't become overcrowded as they grow. You can either do this by giving the seedlings are gentle tug, or take a pair of scissors and snip off the unwanted seedlings at ground level.

You may need to go along the row and re-seed where germination has been erratic. The biggest problem with growing in the ground outdoors is that you can't control the conditions. If the temperature drops or it rains for a week the seeds may rot in the soil or get washed away. The good news is as the temperatures warm up any seeds popped in any gaps will quickly catch up to the ones sown earlier.

TAKE NOTE

WHAT IS GOING ON IN YOUR GARDEN THIS WEEK?

What mulch have you used? What are the common weeds reappearing in your garden? How long are you spending in the garden each day?

....

....

....

....

....

....

....

....

....

THE IMPORTANCE OF FEEDING YOUR PLANTS

Now that your plants are in the ground and about to start producing veggies for you, it is a good time to give them a little boost. Your plants should be looking great at the moment with lots of lush green growth, due to the fact they were started off in a great soil that was well prepared.

But we need to keep the plants happy as they start to give up the goods. Some are hungrier than others and are referred to as gross feeders and they will be the ones who are more in need of a feed as they begin to use up the goodness in the soil.

Some plants really appreciate a good feed as they grow into quite large plants and are in the garden for a long time. Some of the others would enjoy a bonus feed, but don't really need it if you have prepared the soil well. The peas and beans shouldn't need much of a feed as they produce their own nitrogen from the soil, by little nodes on their roots.

Very hungry plants
Beetroot, cabbage, cauliflower, celery, , cucumbers, garlic, pepper, potatoes, pumpkins, silverbeet, spinach, squash, sweetcorn, tomatoes.

Hungry plants
Brussels sprouts, carrots, leeks, lettuce, onions, turnips.

Not so hungry
Beans, peas, radishes.

Generally, the best time to feed the plants is as they begin to flower or produce the edible bits. You need to think about what the plants are doing – if you feed with a high nitrogen feed then the leaves will have an incredible growth spurt at the expense of the fruit and flowers. A balanced feed like the fertiliser and blood and bone you put on the soil at the beginning is a good idea as a top up. Or you can buy a liquid feed which is balanced for growing veggies.

Powder
If you are going use powdered fertilizers then apply it around the base of the plant allowing for the spread of the roots – to about 30cm – **but not** up around the stem as this could damage it. Gently mix the fertilizer into the soil, but try not to disturb the roots and then water the soil well so the nutrients will be taken into the soil where it would be needed. Don't use too much fertilizer as this can

If something is looking a bit peaky or if it has been attacked by pests or there are a lot of pests hanging around, a good feed can help the plant to fight off what ails them.

The key to healthy plants is taking the time in the spring to prepare good soil to last the season. If you don't do this, then your plants will struggle to find good nutrients as the season progresses and your harvest would be compromised.

Beetroot are very hungry plants.

damage the roots with a chemical burn effect. Follow the instructions on the packet.

Liquid

There are a lot of prepared liquid feeds on the market and all you need to do is, following the instructions, add the solution to water in a watering can and give your plants a good drink. Some even have specific plants in mind – such as tomatoes.

Natural

There are lots of natural alternatives out there like compost tea and comfrey solutions and other organic methods that allow you to make a great tonic for your plants. Many involve soaking plants for a couple of weeks in a bucket of water and it can be quite stinky! If you are going to do this, then do your research for further advice as you need to make sure the resulting solution is not too strong and is balanced, as even natural things can cause harm.

A worm farm is a great addition for

TAKE NOTE
WHAT IS GOING ON IN YOUR GARDEN THIS WEEK?

What are you feeding your plants? How often are you feeding them? Are any nearby trees shading your garden now they are full of leaves? Have you harvested anything yet? Have you seen your first flowers or immature fruit?

....

....

....

....

....

free fertilizer as the waste matter from the worms is supposed to be a fantastic pick-me-up for plants.

CONTAINER GROWING

If you are growing your plants in containers, then you need to be more diligent with the feeding as your plant is entirely reliant on you for the nutrients as there is only a finite amount of goodness in the meagre amount of soil in the container and the roots aren't able to go looking for more food as they would in the soil. A liquid feed applied regularly is probably best in this situation.

Nitrogen fixing nodules on pea roots.

SUCCESSION PLANTING

Now is great time to look to the future. Many plants grown in the garden are there for the whole season and will continue to give you something to eat all summer long, or take all season to produce anything, although the rewards here are definitely worth the wait.

Other plants, once they are eaten, they're gone. These are often the crops that reach maturity the quickest. These are also the perfect plants for succession planting. This is when you sow a few seeds often throughout the growing season to ensure a continual supply.

Lettuce, coriander, spinach, carrots, spring onions, sweetcorn, beetroot and all the brassicas are perfect candidates for this. Lettuce, coriander and spinach struggle in the heat of summer and it is generally the tender young leaves that are the best to eat. These plants often bolt to seed readily if conditions aren't perfectly suited and the lettuce in particular can become quite bitter. By sowing enough to feed your family for about three weeks every three weeks will mean you will always have some in the garden. There is nothing worse than having a great row of salad leaves in your garden all planted at the same time and not being able to eat them all, only to find a couple of weeks later you have no salad at all.

Check the recommended growing times for different varieties of your favourite vegetables. Some will prefer cooler or warmer conditions and so you should be able to extend your harvest to cover a good part of the year and in some cases it may be possible to grow all year round.

Spring onions, carrots, beetroot and brassicas take longer to become ready, but they are so quick to eat. Once again by sowing short rows to match how much your family eats every three to four weeks throughout the growing season then you will always have some at the ready.

To avoid a glut of sweetcorn you can plant a new block two to three weeks apart, but to avoid disappointment make sure you don't leave it too late in the season to start them off. Sweetcorn generally takes up to fourteen weeks so find out when you are likely to expect your first frost in the autumn and count back and maybe add a couple more weeks, just to be on the safe side.

TRAINING YOUR PLANTS TO GROW WHERE YOU WANT THEM TO

Tiny seedlings soon become big plants with a mind of their own. It may be your intention that they will grow neatly up the trellis you have thoughtfully provided. Plants often have other ideas and loll about on the ground, cling onto the plants in the next row or just lean on the trellis waving their tendrils helplessly in the air. They often need a little help about now to get growing in the right direction.

Firstly, be very gentle. You don't want to snap the growing tip off.

Growth can be directed by carefully weaving growing tips through trellis and netting. Beans can be encouraged up poles by winding them around their stake. Beans grow in an anticlockwise direction as they follow the sun. Pumpkins and zucchini can be gently persuaded to grow in a certain direction if you carefully lift the growing tip and lay it in the direction you want it to grow. It is best to do this in small movements frequently, rather than trying to lift a long heavy limb and risk snapping it. This is a great way to keep paths clear from rampant growth.

Pumpkins, peas, cucumbers and melons are more than happy to grow vertically and come equipped with strong tendrils to assist them with this.

Other plants don't have a climbing nature but grow tall and need support. Peppers, chillies and capsicums don't grow very tall, but have quite fragile branches. The weight of the fruit can make the plant lean awkwardly or even snap the branches. Tomatoes can grow taller than you and laden with fruit they can be quite heavy and need support to remain upright. The best way to support these plants is by tying them to a sturdy stake or structure with a soft tie. String or wire will cut into the stem

Regular replanting will ensure a great harvest all season.

Tomato laterals can be planted in good rich soil and water well, or put in a jar of water and roots will form and you can have a new plant in no time at all. The plant will be at an advanced state of maturity and will put out flowers quicker than growing from seed.

TAKE NOTE
WHAT IS GOING ON IN YOUR GARDEN THIS WEEK?

What succession plants have you sown? Write down all the details. What support structures are you using? How are your plants responding to them? Has there been much rain?

and weaken the plant. It is best to wrap the tie around the plant, twist it a couple of times and then tie it to the support so there a soft layer between them to avoid damage by rubbing together. But don't tie too tight.

A cage or frame structure is also a great way to provide support as the plants have something lean on.

TAKE OUT TOMATO LATERALS

There are varying opinions about this one – but generally the most common method here is to take out the laterals so the plant doesn't grow too bushy and improves air circulation and allows the plant to focus of fruit not foliage. Laterals are the shoots that grow in the leaf joints between the stems. All you need to do is pinch them out with your thumb and finger. Although I would try and stay on top of your laterals as once they get bigger than a pencil in thickness it can damage the plant to remove them and allow disease to creep in. Also keep an eye on the joints where you have already removed laterals as they can come back.

Don't take them from the dense growth at the top of the plant as it is quite easy to mistake a lateral for the central leader (main shoot) and if you take this out then the plant will stop growing.

WHAT TO DO NOW

This can be an unexciting time in the garden – everything has been planted, or is close to being planted, the weeds are so small and if you've kept on top of them the moment they raise their heads, then there isn't much serious weeding to be done. A good mulch is helping keep the weeds at bay and doing a great job to assist with keeping the soil moist between your consistent watering.

At this time of year there isn't much to harvest yet. This month is often referred to as The Hungry Gap as there isn't a lot to eat and stores from the previous season will have been mostly used up.

However, there are things you can be doing.

Keeping the area beyond the garden tidy and weed-free can really help to minimise the pests, diseases and problems that like to lurk there. Removing hiding places where slugs and snails can loiter will help to give you an upper hand against these voracious pests. Pulling out weeds that readily spread their seeds will help reduce the introduction of weeds into the garden and remove opportunity for pests such as aphids to build up unnoticed in large numbers before invading your garden. And keeping things in order around the garden will make it look nice too.

Quite a versatile plant, our humble pea.

WHEN CAN I EAT MY PEAS?

Peas are a great staple to have in the garden in the spring and autumn months. The sweet round peas are a secret growing away, hidden in the pods, developing a sweet rich flavour but how do you know when it a good time to eat them?

The good news is if you are impatient you don't need to wait for the actual peas. The tender young tips and tendrils can be nipped out of the top of the plant and gobbled

The more you pick the more you get.

Peas are such a versatile crop

up in a salad with a lovely fresh dressing. The tendrils can be a bit woody if they are too old, but the tips are delicious. This also helps the plant as you will find that the growing tip is replaced by a couple of new shoots and therefore there will be more peas at the end of the day.

You can also eat the flowers too when they show up... But for every flower you eat then there is one less pea pod developing.

Following on from that, the developing pea pod can be eaten at any stage and all pea varieties can be treated as snow peas or mangetout and can be used in salads and stir-fries. Although this delightful pleasure can't last forever. As the peas begin to form inside the pod the inside wall thickens and becomes a bit stringy and so it isn't as nice to eat.

Then you have to wait until the pods begin to fatten up. Once they begin to become like little green cylinders then they are good to go. Open a few to see what stage they are at – there is nothing to lose if you do it too early – there will be more peas coming along. The ideal size is when they fill the pod but haven't begun to 'square off' as they grow up against each other. It should take roughly 8–11 weeks from planting the seed.

Fresh peas are so sweet, juicy and delicious and the best thing to do is to pick them every day. The more you pick, the more will grow. But you have to remember that the plant has a different agenda to you. While you are looking for a nice veggie to go with your mashed potato, the plant is looking at making seeds so it can grow hundreds of new plants. So if you leave pods on the plant they will reach a point when they are no longer nice to eat. The sugars begin to convert to starch and they become hard and have a bit of a metallic taste. You can tell which peas have gone too far as the pods begin to go wrinkly and then they start to go yellow. But more importantly, the plant will think it has done its job and stop growing new pods – so make sure you get every last one of them when you are out there with your basket.

Waste not want not. Aside from putting the shelled pea pods on the compost pile they can also be used to make pea pod soup or even pea pod wine…

TAKE NOTE
WHAT IS GOING ON IN YOUR GARDEN THIS WEEK?

Has anything started to flower? Have you managed to harvest anything yet? How long are you spending in the garden each day?
Take some photos and compare them to when you last took photos to see how much the garden has grown in such a short time.

EARLY SUMMER

Finally, the season that everyone loves arrives. Hot, sunny days that last well into the evening, making outdoor living so pleasurable. As a gardener this is fabulous news, no more working in the fading light, in chilly conditions. The bees begin to buzz about the garden in earnest as more and more of your crops begin to bear flowers. Early summer is a lovely time in the garden as the plants begin to fill out and it starts to look like a well-organised growing space that you can't help but be proud of all you have achieved so far.

Sow	*Plant*	*Maintain*	*Harvest*
• Outdoors – beans, beetroot, broccoli, Brussels sprouts, cabbage, carrot, cauliflower, celery, cucumber, eggplant, leek, melon, spring onion, parsnip, pepper, pumpkin, radish, silverbeet, squash, sweetcorn, tomato and zucchini.	• Plant seedlings of beans, beetroot, broccoli, cabbage, cauliflower, celery, cucumber, eggplant, lettuce, melon, pepper, pumpkin, spinach, squash, sweetcorn, tomato and zucchini.	• Regular deep watering is best. • Remove laterals from tomatoes. • Thin carrots. • Remove weeds while they are small. • Feed plants weekly or fortnightly with a liquid feed. • Keep an eye out for pests and disease – be prepared to act quickly! • Harvest daily.	• Asparagus, beans, beetroot, cabbage, carrot, cucumber, garlic, lettuce, onion, potato, peas, radish, shallots, silverbeet, spring onion, spinach, squash, strawberries, tomato and zucchini NOTE: This is just a guide – things may happen faster or slower in your garden.
• Succession sow – beetroot, broccoli, carrot, lettuce, radish, spring onion and sweetcorn every 3 weeks or so.			

Lush tender leaves are vulnerable to pests

FLOWERS

As you look about your garden and see your thriving plants you will notice an abundance of flowers adding a touch of colour to your green garden. Aside from making the garden look pretty, they are very important as they will become the fruit you harvest later or contribute to it.

Some plants such as peas, beans, tomatoes, peppers and their relatives are self-fertile. This means they can pollinate themselves within the flower without too much help. Tapping the stalk just above the flower can encourage the pollen to fall.

Others like the cucumber, zucchini, pumpkin and squash need two flowers – male ones and female ones. The pollen from the male flower needs to get to a female flower so they can make baby zucchinis. This is usually done by bees. The male flowers tend to jump the gun a bit and the first two or three flowers are males and without the female flowers there will be no produce.

If you don't see any bees about the place you can do it yourself. You take a male flower first thing in the morning and take off the petals and then take it to the female flower and rub the male part on female part at the centre of the flowers. You can tell a male flower because the stem is straight and goes straight into the flower. However, the female flower has a small swelling under the flower, at the end of the stem and if this is pollinated it will turn into the fruit.

If tomato leaves are in contact with the ground then it doesn't hurt the plant to cut them off, to reduce the risk of pest and disease.

BEES

The ideal situation is to have the bees work their pollination magic in your garden and so the aim is to encourage them into your garden by making it bee friendly. As bees dance across your flowers they are looking for two things: the sweet nectar for energy and the pollen to balance out their diet. So it makes sense then to plant the kind of flowers in and around your garden that bees actually like to eat from.

Planting flowers in large groups will be more effective in attracting them rather than one or two plants dotted about the place, but if space is limited you can only do what you can. It would be ideal to plant flowers of all shapes and sizes that flourish throughout the

Tomato plants should also be growing quite vigorously now too, so pinch out those laterals and keep tying them to the stakes as they grow.

TAKE NOTE

WHAT IS GOING ON IN YOUR GARDEN THIS WEEK?

What bee attracting flowers do you have in your garden? Are you seeing bees pollinating your crops? What is being harvested? How much have you harvested? Do you like the flavours?

entire season to give the bees a reason to keep coming back. But bees do have a few preferences and love blue, purple, violet, white, and yellow above other colours.

Bees should be encouraged into your garden.

If you are going to spray pesticides when the bad bugs get too much, make sure you follow the instructions on the packet, avoid spraying directly on flowers. Bees generally don't fly at temperatures lower than 10°C or at night so if you must spray then very early in the day or late at night will reduce the harm done to these vital pollinators.

WHEN CAN I EAT MY GARLIC?

Garlic is one of those sneaky underground growers. As a new gardener I was surprised to find that they form such crisp white bulbs in the dirt – I would never have guessed it.

If you are growing the hard-neck variety, there is a special treat to be had from the flower stalk that pops up in spring. It is edible and can be used in a pesto, stir-fried or pickled and it is in the best interests of the garlic to pick them as they take energy from the growing bulb.

So there they are – mostly under the ground, doing their thing for a very long time, roughly six months. The old wives' tale says 'plant on the shortest day and harvest on the longest day'. Which is a pretty good indicator, however as it isn't the only day that you can plant the garlic, it isn't the only day to harvest it either. It can be planted from late autumn to early spring, depending on your climate. So for a successful harvest, find out when is best for your garden.

Once zucchini get going, check daily to avoid monsters – and check thoroughly as they are great at hiding.

So how can you tell when it is ready?

It is handy to mark the expected harvest date on your calendar, but as with everything seasonal weather variations can make a bit of a difference between too early and too late. If you pull them up too soon then the garlic cloves will be too small – still edible, but fiddly to peel and considering they can get bigger if left longer, this can be a bit of a disappointment. If you are too late then you can affect the ability to store it for the months to come. The protective layers can perish and the cloves themselves begin to shrivel and you won't have plump tight bulb. If you leave it too long, it won't be worth eating.

Look at the leaves. The lower third form the top part of the protective layers around the cloves so when they are brown and drying out it is about right.

Don't pull it up by the stalk because if you break it you will compromise its ability to be stored. Gently dig it up by going alongside – but not too close then lift from underneath.

Allow it to dry in a shaded, well ventilated space as the sun can damage the garlic and deteriorate the flavour and reduce the quality of the bulb.

Plump Garlic. Photo credit Lynda Scott.

SURVIVING THE HOLIDAYS

Just when the plants need us the most and the harvest is just starting to get going, we dive head first into the summer holiday season that leaves us with little time for the gardening. The garden can become quite neglected at this time of year, however if you want to have something to come back to afterward then you need to put in place a few measures to ensure the garden survives without you.

Weeds

Firstly, it is important to keep the weeds down leading up to the beginning of the neglectful season. If you have been keeping on top of them anyway and removing them while they are little this will really help. It is amazing how quickly weeds can grow at this time of year. It is very important not to let them set seed or those seeds will be weeds by the time you come back from holiday. Thousands of weeds.

Weeding the veggie garden should be on the list of things to do before you go away, not only to make it easier on yourself when it all goes back to normal, but weeds can reduce the airflow in your garden and therefore increase

Remove every weed you see.

the susceptibility of fungal disease for your plants, and as you won't have time to give the garden regular feeds, the weeds will be stealing from the mouths of your babes!

Water

This is the life blood of the garden. Without it all will die. It isn't advisable to rely on the rain to water your garden. During the holiday season you need a good plan.

An irrigation system can be put together easily enough using sprinklers, sprayers, soaker hoses and drippers that can be found at most garden centres. The components themselves are quite inexpensive. If you are unsure of what you need, talk to the staff,

they are quite knowledgeable. For a small garden this is easy enough to do. Although for a larger garden it can start to get pricey.

A tap on a timer to go on and off for 20 minutes or so every other day will ensure your garden will be able to survive.

Failing this you could have a friendly neighbour or friend to come over to wave the hose around. Choose this person wisely as, many who are willing don't understand the exact needs of the garden and may not water deep enough or the leaves of the tomato get a bit of a soak followed by a bit of blight.

The last option is self-watering. Poke pin holes in the bottom of plastic bottles and burying them beside the plants so the holes are in the root zone. Ideally this should have been done when you plant the plants so you don't damage the roots, but if you have no other option it is better than killing them by desiccation. The longer you are going away the bigger the bottle. For plants in containers fill a wine bottle with water and then quickly turn it upside down and push it into the soil. The water will leak out slowly and should give you at least a weekend.

Before you go away, give the garden a good deep soak so the soil is wet to a depth that would make it hard for a drying wind to get to.

Mow the lawns – it doesn't take long for grass to set seeds – they seem to know they are up against it and try and get in before the mower comes out again. The last thing you want is to have them blown into your garden causing a weedy nightmare.

HARVEST

Harvest anything that is remotely edible. Do a hard pick or it will just go to waste. If the broccoli, peas or beans look nearly ready then pick them because they won't wait for you and after months of nurturing the last thing you want is to miss the edible stage! If the tomato looks almost red, then pick it. It will ripen on a windowsill. You can also eat small cucumbers.

A minder who is watering in exchange for food, often won't know how to harvest properly and will only pick what they see or what they need and you will come home to yellow cucumbers and marrows that were hidden in the undergrowth or peas that are past it.

It isn't just about the wasted food – although this is a shame. But it is about the message being sent to the plant. They are there to set seed. And once they achieve this goal then generally they shut up shop. The job is done. As hungry gardeners it is our aim to eat as much as we can from each plant and so we need to keep the plant thinking it is a failure as they are quite tenacious and will try, try and try again until after months they die in an exhausted heap in cooling autumn weather. To leave even a single pea pod will tell the plant they have done it and their progeny will live on.

Set up an automated irrigation system.

FEED

After being in the ground for so long, the plant will have made quite a dent in the rich store of nutrients you have provided for them. To give them a liquid feed or a side dressing of a slow-release fertiliser at this point will give a pick-me-up and help them to stay strong and healthy until you get back.

PESTS AND DISEASE

Look over your garden thoroughly. If you spot an aphid, don't think "oh, it's only one", squash it or you will come home to one million and the life sucked out of your plant. If you are in any doubt about it, give your garden a quick spray with a food safe pesticide to slow them down enough that you can deal with it when you get back. Once summer really gets going, so do the pests!

TAKE NOTE
WHAT IS GOING ON IN YOUR GARDEN THIS WEEK?

Write down what you did to prepare for going on holiday. When you come home make a note of the weather while you were away and how your garden fared in your absence and record anything you may want to do differently next year.

TIDY UP

This is a good time to do a bit of general maintenance as well. Check your stakes and structures to make sure they are still strong and sturdy. Pop in extra support now if you are unsure. There is nothing more heartbreaking than coming back from the holidays to find all your stakes broken under the weight of the tomatoes and your plants bruised and contorted on the ground. Tie in any plants that need it, nip off any laterals. Remove some lower leaves to increase airflow.

COMMON PESTS

Unfortunately, you are not the only one out there who wants to eat your crops. You will find your garden turning into a battlefield as the summer progresses as most of the pest populations will grow incrementally until eventually they are taken out by the frost. Although often the next generation will be biding its time hidden about the garden waiting for next season.

Here are the top 10 most common creatures you may encounter in your garden. This isn't a comprehensive list as there are others, and some just specific to your area, so if you come across something not on the list, you should be able to find specific advice locally.

1. **Aphids / Greenfly** can bother most plants in your garden – once they spot a weakness then they are in there and sucking the life out of your plants. Be vigilant and check your plants regularly. An infestation can go from a few to thousands in a matter of days. Squashing them and or a strong blast with the hose can see them off. Or take to them with a chemical remedy such as pyrethrum or a stronger solution for a really bad infestation.

2. **The carrot fly** is a particularly nasty pest. He finds your carrot through smell, and so make sure you remove all trace of carrot thinning's from the

Shield Bug eggs.

Caterpillars come in many kinds.

immediate area, and try not to damage any carrots unnecessarily. He will lay eggs near the carrot and the little worm will burrow into the carrot and then eat away at the carrot causing poor growth. A horticultural fleece cloth can prevent the carrot fly landing on your crop. Or if you experience an infestation, next season plant onion or chives beside your carrots as it is supposed to confuse them. Apparently they don't like to fly up so you can put a physical solid barrier around your carrot row at about 60 cm and you will be fine.

You can still eat the carrot – just chop the damaged bit off and take extra precautions next season.

3. **Caterpillars** have a few different types that enjoy feasting on your garden and are the juvenile stage of moths and butterflies. Keep an eye out for them on your crops and check under the leaves for eggs. Often holes in the leaves and caterpillar droppings are an obvious sign you have a problem. The best course of action is to just pick them off. There are other chemical solutions, so investigate which ones suit you and your garden.

4. **Cutworms** can be quite annoying. They are the juvenile stage of a moth that lays its eggs in the soil. When they hatch they make a bee line for your seedlings and chew them off at ground level. You won't often see them

You don't want to find Shield Bugs doing this – squash them!

A White Cabbage caterpillar can decimate your brassicas.

unless you go out at night with a torch because they are active under the cover of darkness and sleep all day. You can protect your seedlings by popping a tube around the base of the plant to create a physical barrier.

5. **Leaf miner** larvae create tunnels inside leaves. And you get crazy patterns on the leaves. The best way to control them is to remove the infected leaves and destroy them. Hang yellow sticky traps to catch any adults flying around.

6. **Green Vegetable Bug** aka Shield Bug or Stink Bug and members of his family are a nuisance and love most of your veggies. You can hear him coming in as when he flies in he sounds like a helicopter that needs a bit of engine work. The best advice is to squash him immediately. Apparently being squashed releases a smell that lets all the other Green Vegetable bugs know that this is not a safe place to be and they all go away – well that is the theory. Nothing beats squishing for satisfaction value, unless you have loads of juveniles running amok on your plants then you may need to look into a suitable chemical treatment. These guys are sap suckers and can seriously harm your plants by sucking too much, causing the plants to wilt, introducing diseases or you could end up with funny shaped crops. They are much more prolific in the warmer weather so

Check your garden every day for the early signs of a pest invasion as numbers can escalate really quickly in the right conditions.

try and squish as many as you can in the early season to help keep numbers down. Maybe have a challenge in the family to keep a squash record with a prize for the winner.

7. **Slugs and snails** can make your newly transplanted plants disappear without a trace on the first night or the fifth or the twelfth. When the plants get bigger they just hide among the leaves. The choice is yours how to cope with these, but I personally prefer slug bait – but don't get it on the plant as you sprinkle it liberally about the place.

8. **Thrips** are a nasty little pest, particularly in greenhouses, but also in the general garden. There are loads of different kinds, but if you have one of them then you have a problem. They are sap suckers and lay hundreds of eggs in flower buds and on young leaves. Because they are so tiny – smaller than 2mm, it is hard to detect but if you have a white mottled leaves and stunted shoots and flowers then this may be the cause. The best way to tackle them is to spray several times to break the life cycle with a product such as a pyrethrum-based pesticide or maybe something a little stronger, yet still safe for edibles.

9. **White cabbage butterfly** is the worst pest for the summer growing brassicas as there are white cabbage butterflies everywhere! They lay their eggs on your

brassica leaves and then these nasty green caterpillars hatch and feast on your plants and may even work their way into the hidden depths of your broccoli or cauliflower to be found by an unsuspecting diner. Check thoroughly before cooking. There are several ways you can combat this and often a combination of these is the best method.

- The first method is exclusion – build a net around your plants to stop the butterfly landing and laying eggs. Or even easier is to buy a mesh pop up laundry hamper and put it upside down over your plants – anchor it down to stop it blowing away.
- Vigilance – go out there every day and check under the leaves for eggs or caterpillars – rub the eggs off with your finger. The butterfly generally only lays one egg per leaf. You may get more eggs laid by different butterflies.
- Decoy – There is a school of thought that if you made little white plastic butterflies and hung them around your brassicas then it would keep the real butterflies away as they are a one at time kind of insect and take turns laying eggs that have the potential to destroy your plant.

10. **White fly** – this guy is normally associated with greenhouses, but he can also be found out in the garden. He is about 3mm long and he and his mates suck the life out of your plants. They can quickly grow to gargantuan proportions and when disturbed a cloud of them will fly from your plants. Yellow sticky traps may help, but the most effective way is to spray – a pyrethrum-based spray is good, but you may need more than one type of spray and alternate as they can become resistant to the sprays quickly as they have a short lifecycle.

TAKE NOTE
WHAT IS GOING ON IN YOUR GARDEN THIS WEEK?

What pests are you finding in your garden? What course of action have you decided to take? Come back here again in a few weeks and record how successful you were and if necessary what other solutions do you try in a brave attempt to keep your garden pest free.

COMMON DISEASES

Pests aren't the only thing attempting to ravage your plants, they are also at great risk of disease. Deal with problems straight away for a better chance of giving your plants a full recovery. Don't leave diseased material lying about and certainly don't put it on your compost heap. Burn it or send it out with the trash. Clean your tools regularly and especially after using them on diseased plants. Even cleaning them between plants is a good idea. Keep on top of weeds in the garden and nearby as they can harbour disease. The other point to remember is starting with a healthy soil will give you healthy plants that will be more resilient to the diseases they encounter. If you do find yourself stricken with disease, avoid planting crops from the same family in the same spot for a good two to three years or things could get a whole lot worse.

Here are the top five diseases you are likely to encounter at some stage in your gardening journey. However they aren't the only ones, so if your plants look poorly then investigate the possible problems and start treatment as soon as you can.

Damping off
This is caused by fungi that live in the soil and affects young seedlings. However, seedlings are mostly at risk of this disease when conditions are ideal for it. If it is too wet, too humid, there is poor airflow and the seedlings are too thickly sown then there is a high chance you will encounter this problem and your seedlings will fall

Blight on tomato leaves.

Blight on a tomato.

over and die. If you don't over-water your plants, make sure they have good airflow and space your seeds well then you have a much better chance of avoiding this disease. Another tip is to water with clean water at the same temperature as the conditions your plants are growing in.

Blight

There are two kinds of this fungal disease. Early blight is terrible. It strikes tomatoes or potatoes quickly – early in the season the plant develops brown patches all over it and if left it will destroy the plant overnight and spread to the other tomato and potato plants and kill them too. There is only one thing for it – to pull up your plants and put them in the rubbish bin – not the compost. Don't leave any trace of the plant in your garden. Don't grow tomatoes in the same spot next year. Late blight is a little better as you have

As with people, the best thing you can do in your garden to prevent disease is to use good hygiene practices.

pretty much had a season of tomatoes from your plants before it strikes, but it is just as devastating and you need to remove the infected plant immediately. You can spray your plants with a copper spray as a preventative.

Rust

You can generally tell if you have this fungal disease as your crop will take on an orange rusty look. When the orange pustules appear the disease is fully blown in your plant and ready to launch a million spores across to the other plants. The good news is each rust is pretty much specific to each crop so the rust on your garlic is different to the rust on your leeks. As with most fungal diseases good airflow can help to prevent infestation in the first place. Good hygiene practices in the garden and a good mulch can prevent spores being splashed up onto the leaves when being

Powdery Mildew.

Treat Powdery Mildew as soon as you see it.

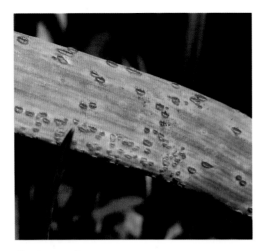

Rust on garlic.

watered can reduce the risk of infection. If you do find yourself with rust, remove the affected leaves and spray with a copper-based spray. This is a stubborn disease and there is a chance you may not win this battle.

Powdery Mildew

In hot, dry weather fungal spores germinate on dry leaf surfaces. It is more common in late summer and will slow down and eventually stop your crop but won't kill it. You can reduce the risk of mildew by keeping the weeds down, the air circulation up and don't water on the leaves – just on the soil but water consistently. You can pick off infected leaves, spray with a fungicide or spray with a diluted milk solution of 30% skim milk 70% water. Or even a baking soda mix of half a teaspoon in 1 litre of water.

Blossom end rot

This isn't so much a disease as an avoidable problem in tomatoes, eggplants, peppers and even squash. The end of the fruit becomes sunken and turns black. It is generally caused by uneven watering and a lack of available calcium in the soil which stops the rapid growth of the fruit in its tracks. It is more common in the beginning of the season as cold soil can impact upon the rate water and nutrients are taken up by the roots. Starting with a well-balanced soil and planting when the soil is warm enough can reduce the risk. If you have the problem, just remove the affected fruit and throw it away and give the plants a liquid feed suitable for tomatoes or fruiting vegetables. The good news is it isn't catching.

Sweetcorn gets quite tall.

MID SUMMER

This is the height of summer when everything comes together. The harvest is in full swing and abundant. The weather is actually mostly nice and the balmy evenings linger well into the night. But more than ever you need to make sure your plants are well watered as generally this is the month that sees the least amount of rain, and any moisture that does land on the soil quickly evaporates away in the heat of the day. The upside is the weeds tend to slow down in their growth. But any that do show themselves, remove them out because they are stealing nutrients, harbouring pests and disease and are generally up to no good. However, the pest numbers begin their steady increase as they revel in the warmer conditions.

Sow

- Outdoors – beans, beetroot, broccoli, Brussels sprouts, cabbage, carrot, cauliflower, celery, cucumber, leek, lettuce, spring onion, parsnip, radish, silverbeet, swede, sweetcorn, turnip and zucchini.

- Succession sow – beetroot, broccoli, carrot, lettuce, radish, spring onion and sweetcorn every 3 weeks or so.

Plant

- Plant seedlings of beans, cucumber, eggplant, melon, pepper, pumpkin, squash, sweetcorn, tomato and zucchini.

Maintain

- Thin carrots.

- Tie in wayward plants.

- Remove bottom leaves from tomatoes to help air circulation.

- Regular deep watering is best.

- Remove laterals from tomatoes.

- Remove weeds while they are small.

- Feed plants weekly or fortnightly with a liquid feed.

- Keep an eye out for pests and disease – be prepared to act quickly!

- Harvest daily.

Harvest

- Beans, beetroot, cabbage, carrot, cucumber, eggplant, garlic, lettuce, onion, potato, radish, shallots, silverbeet, spinach, spring onion, squash, sweetcorn, strawberries, tomato and zucchini.

NOTE: This is just a guide – things may happen faster or slower in your garden.

The bees are at their busiest in a midsummer garden.

WHAT'S GOING ON?

Tomatoes

These should well be on the way to towering above you. Make sure you keep it tied in to whatever structure you decided to go with. A truss of tomatoes near peak perfection can be quite heavy and can easily break unsupported branches. Also remove any of the old and tired leaves near the bottom of the plant to improve airflow. If your tomatoes don't have good airflow, they are at risk of blight.

You should be starting to get some lovely red fruit – if not by now then soon. Watch out for the birds – they love them too.

Cucumbers

You should have plenty by now. Keep the plants hydrated as cucumbers are mostly water and it has to come from somewhere. Also remove some of the older leaves to improve airflow as without good airflow you can get powdery mildew – it doesn't kill the plant, just slows it down considerably. Try not to splash the leaves when watering.

Peas

These should be well and truly over by now. You should be able to sow more in late summer, early autumn when the weather starts to cool down.

Carrots

These should be a good size to eat now and if you haven't sown a new row or two then now is time to pop some in. Actually any time is a good time to sow carrots – just keep the soil moist while they germinate. Laying a plank of wood over the row for a couple of weeks should do the trick.

Zucchini

Check your plants every day and do a good look because they are great at hiding. You can remove some of the older leaves on the zucchini too as it is also at risk of powdery mildew.

Tomatoes are maturing.

Beans

You should also be getting a great crop of beans. The key with these is the more you pick the more you get, so stay on top of your harvesting for a great crop.

Peppers and chillies

These should be slowly growing and you may or may not be seeing flowers and if you are lucky, there should be a fruit or two. The key to these is the heat, so if they have been languishing in the garden, the more settled weather you normally get from now on should see them flourishing.

Salad

If you aren't already you should be popping in new plants every couple of weeks and there is no shame in garden centre seedlings. Leafy salad plants don't actually like the hot weather and will quickly go bitter and try to go to seed so the key to it all is to replace them with tender young plants often.

Now is a good time to plant another batch of potatoes. They should be ready well before the first frost, with a bit of luck.

WHEN CAN I EAT MY SWEETCORN?

This is a massive plant. It spends all summer growing visibly bigger before your very eyes, yet the edible bit is hidden away, carefully wrapped in layers of green leaves, leaving us to only guess when it will be ready.

One thing I found a little disappointing as a new gardener was with such a huge plant that there was only one cob, or at best two. Very rarely would you get three. But all is forgiven once you taste fresh sweetcorn straight off the plant – oh my goodness,

Sweetcorn ready to eat.

like nothing from a store. So sweet and juicy.

But in order to taste all that sweet juiciness you need to know when is the optimum time to pluck it from the plant. But you also need to know a little about the plant. The tassels at the top of the plant release the pollen onto the silks that poke out of the top of the cob or ear of sweetcorn. This is why it is best to plant the sweetcorn in a block instead of a row, so there is the best chance of each silk coming in contact with pollen.

The quicker you get the sweetcorn from the plant to the pot, the sweeter it will be. Fresh sweetcorn is a delicious treat for all the family.

This is because each silk is attached to each kernel in the cob. If you find a blank space or two in your cob it is because its silk missed being pollinated, but it's no big deal to be missing one or two. The silk is the key to when your sweetcorn is ready.

It should change from a pale shiny yellow to a crispy, dry brown, but as it is a little tricky to decide how brown is brown, there are a couple of other tips to confirm your decision to harvest.

❉ Give the cob a good feel. Through the husk it should be fat and firm up and down the entire length of the ear. It should feel like a shop-bought one.

❉ As the cob grows fat it should begin to stick out from the stalk at a greater angle than before.

❉ And then finally you can open it up at the top and have a look. If the kernels look fat and yellow, you can check if they are actually ready by piercing one with your fingernail. The juice should look a little milky. If it is clear, then the sweetcorn needs a little longer so wrap the husk back up and try again in a couple of days. If there isn't much juice at all and the kernels look a little puckered, then you have left it too long.

NOT ALL INSECTS ARE BAD

With increasing pest populations loitering about on your precious plants it can seem like an automatic reaction to get rid of them all. However in nature there is balance and for every nasty bug in your garden there is generally another one wanting to eat it. And then there are of course the pollinators – without them there is no fruit. So before you grab the spray gun and do a spot of extermination, have a close look and see if you have friends in there amongst the foes.

The most common beneficial insects that can be found or attracted to your garden include:

Hoverflies

They look like small bees that dart and hover about the garden. The great thing is their eggs are laid near aphid infestations and the larvae feed on them and get fat, while the parents are sipping nectar and pollinating plants.

Lacewings

These have hungry larvae and are said to look a little like an alligator, with pincers to attack their prey. They really aren't fussy and will eat about 200 of your common garden pests a week.

Praying mantis

These are good friends in the garden and are definitely what can be called predatory insects as they munch and crunch their way around the garden. The only problem is they aren't discerning in their choice of prey and will just as happily eat a caterpillar one moment and a lacewing the next.

Ladybirds do such great work in the garden.

Ladybirds

This cute little bug is a fabulous friend to have in the garden as it loves to eat aphids and other small insects. In its lifetime it can eat up to 5000 aphids. Unfortunately, it isn't as well recognised in its juvenile stage and can often be mistaken for a pest.

Ground beetles

These beetles can come in many colours depending on where you live and scuttle about in the leaf litter and using their sharp jaws, gobble up slugs, cutworms and other soil pests. You can't argue that something that eats pests is a friend indeed.

Wasps

These aren't often seen as friends in the garden – mostly because some can be a bit aggressive. However, they do have their value, particularly the parasitic wasps who lay their eggs in caterpillars which results in the death of the caterpillar. Wasps actually eat caterpillars and other insects or take them to their nests for their young, particularly early in the season before they switch to the sweet stuff.

Spiders

They spin their webs about the garden to catch and eat insects so they have to be one of the good guys. Unfortunately, they aren't very discriminating and eat whoever gets stuck in the web. Although they may eat their share of other beneficial insects they are generally considered welcome in the garden.

Frogs can eat more than their fair share of slugs.

Frogs and toads

Creating an environment to attract these into the garden can only work in your favour as they love to eat slugs and other insect pests.

This is not a comprehensive list by a long shot and there are many more helpful bugs out there. You may even find some specific to your area. So take the time to find out just who is lurking in your garden and what they look like at all stages of their life cycle, so you don't accidentally kill them. Insects are more than just creepy crawlies – many of them are our allies in the battle of the veggies.

WHEN CAN I EAT MY PEPPERS?

These plants have their fruit right there in front of us, amongst their leaves and branches. And yet there is still this dilemma – when do I pick them? Especially the green ones, they may look big enough, but are they ready to eat?

The good news is they can be eaten at all stages and the ideal size for a green bell pepper is from about 8cm. However, they do taste the very best when they are mature and completely ripe. With the chillies, the heat also increases with increased maturity.

Peppers and chillies come in such a wide range of colours, but they all start out green and can be eaten green, but then depending on what you have planted the peppers will change into their final colour as they ripen. Yellow peppers come from the yellow variety and aren't an intermediate stage for the red ones.

Of course there is the all-important record

After handling chillies DON'T TOUCH YOURSELF ANYWHERE!

keeping. If you mark on the calendar the expected harvest date from planting the seed, it will give you a good idea, however variations in the weather will either slow down or speed up the actual time to harvest.

Peppers can be eaten anytime.

Some chillies can give you a bit of a clue as to when they are ready. They get little cracks on their skins when they ready. This is called 'corking'.

Take care while harvesting your peppers as the plants may look robust but they are actually quite fragile and one wrong move and you could break off a whole branch instead of a single pepper. To be on the safe side use a pair of scissors. This can also protect your fingers from the hot oils of the chillies.

To ensure the plant keeps producing peppers all season long, pick the peppers as soon as they are big enough, and don't worry about what seems like taking too many green ones, as the more you pick the more will grow and there will be more than enough red ones later in the season.

There is nothing like a fresh pepper. It is so juicy and fresh and when you cut through it with a knife it is as crispy as a freshly picked apple and makes a great crunchy sound.

WHAT IS GOING ON NOW

You should be trying to get into the garden every day now. Check for pests and disease and tackle them as soon as you see them. This will ensure your garden stays healthy. You should also be deeply watering your thirsty garden as the heat of summer will be taking its toll.

Any wayward growth on tall or climbing plants should be tucked in or tied in to prevent damage from a strong summer breeze or being snapped from heavily laden branches. Giving hungry plants a feed is a good idea as the soil will be starting to get tired and the plants will need a bit extra when they are fruiting.

STORING THE HARVEST

This is the season of abundance and you will find you are becoming inundated with produce. The much-anticipated first zucchini or tomato was lovingly cherished, but now they can become a little overwhelming. So the question needs to be asked: What to do with it all?

You can generously share your abundance with friends, family and neighbours and even the local food bank would welcome what you can't manage to eat.

So your harvest doesn't go to waste, make sure it is stored properly. This can extend its shelf life and allow you to enjoy the fruits of your labour – in some cases well into winter. Spending time in the kitchen is just as much a part of vegetable gardening as digging over the dirt in spring.

The Fridge

Some vegetables just aren't meant to be kept in the fridge. Tomatoes, potatoes and onions can go soft or have their flavour altered in a undesirable way.

Most fruit give off ethylene gas, which is a normal plant hormone that encourages ripening. However, if these fruit are stored with most vegetables side by side in the fridge then the vegetables are more likely

Whip up a large batch of pasta sauce.

*Pack tomatoes off
to the freezer.*

to go off quicker.
It is best to store
these separately in
your fridge.

Humidity is a key
factor in the longevity
of vegetables stored
in the fridge. Too
much moisture can
cause the larger
vegetables like carrots
and zucchini to go
off and not enough
moisture can cause
the thinner vegetable
such as spinach and

*Don't
harvest in
the rain.*

broccoli to wilt. Storing your
vegetables separately based
on their likelihood to wilt
in the fridge can lengthen
the time they stay fresh
in there.

The Freezer

This is a great way to take care of the
harvest for long-term storage. If vegetables
are properly prepared and the freezer
stays frozen, then vegetables can last up
to 12 months – in time for next season's
inundation.

The vegetables will benefit from being
prepared for the freezer as soon after
harvesting as possible. However, there is
great debate about how to prepare the
vegetables for freezing and the question is:
To blanch or not to blanch.

Blanching is plunging into boiling
water for a few moments to slow the
enzymes that ripen the vegetables, and
preserve the flavour, colour and texture.
Then immediately plunge them into icy
cold water to stop the cooking process. The
time in the boiling water varies depending
on what you are trying to blanch, working
in small batches gives the best results.

Adding salt to the blanching water
can help to retain the nutrients in the
vegetables.

However, this can make some
vegetables quite soggy.
So you need to make
sure you dry them
thoroughly before
freezing. Cooking
from frozen is also
a good practice.

*Good
airflow is
important around
stored vegetables.*

Hang onions in a cool, dry place.

Some vegetables freeze just as well without the need for blanching, for example sweetcorn, tomatoes and peppers, although the peppers and tomatoes will be mushy on defrosting so are more suited to cooking than salads.

At the end of the day this may come down to personal choice and what works best for you.

When freezing your vegetables, put them in freeze-safe bags and try to remove as much air as possible to avoid freezer burn.

Waste not want not, any damaged veggies or ones approaching the 'too old' stage should be eaten first – just chop off any bad bits. They won't be suitable for long-term storage.

and isn't too difficult. It works by lowering the moisture content to a point that food spoilage bugs can't grow. However, unless you live in a dry desert, using just the sun may not be as successful as you'd hope.

Investing in an electric dehydrator may be a worthwhile option if you want to do a lot of dehydrating, or for just a one-off then the oven set to low can do a good job.

It may not suit all vegetables, but offers the benefit of taking up less storage space and doesn't need ongoing energy to be stored.

Dehydrating

This is the oldest form of food preservation

Store potatoes in a cool, dark place.

In the Shed

Some vegetables are robust enough to have great keeping properties and only need to be kept in a cool, dry shed with great airflow. Pumpkins benefit from a wash first, but potatoes, onion and garlic prefer just to have the soil brushed off.

It isn't recommended to store them in plastic as this can cause them to sweat and then rot. Don't allow them to touch each other and check often and remove any that don't seem to be keeping well before they ruin the rest.

Into Jars

There is a wide range of possibilities such as pickling, jam making, bottling and canning. These require a lot more attention to detail as there is a greater risk of food poisoning if you don't do it correctly. But is worth giving it a go as there so many wonderful and delicious solutions to your over-abundant harvest. Just make sure you investigate the techniques thoroughly and follow the instructions in the recipe exactly.

TAKE NOTE
WHAT IS GOING ON IN YOUR GARDEN THIS WEEK?

How much are you harvesting? What are you doing with your excess crop? What are your favourite ways to store the harvest?

....

....

....

....

WHEN CAN I EAT MY MELONS?

It is always exciting to see melons growing larger by the day in your garden and waiting for the right time can seem to take forever. Harvesting too early can result in disappointment, so the pressing question is, how to tell when they are ready?

There are many varieties of melon out there and they all have their subtle little signs to alert the gardener that it is time to harvest, but basically they fall into one of two groups: the rough-skinned melons that look like they have a kind of netting over them and the smooth-skinned varieties.

✻ The rough-skinned ones are easy to tell when they are ready as they will come off the vine without any pulling or tugging required. Another good indication is the bottom of the melon where it has been sitting on the ground turns yellow. They should also smell lovely and sweet.

How can you tell when this is ready?

Make sure you harvest your melons at the peak of ripeness as they will get softer on storage, but they won't get any sweeter.

❋ The smooth-skinned ones aren't as easy to tell, but you should never pull one of these from the vine, cut them off or they will become susceptible to rotting quicker than normal – that is if you don't intend to eat them there and then!

   If the skin is hairy it isn't ready yet. A ripe smooth skin melon should feel a little waxy. The skin should also change colour and be less green. Some varieties change completely but others just become a lighter shade of green so it pays to watch your melons as they develop. You may also notice the bottom turning yellow where it has been sitting on the ground. The other giveaway is of course the wonderful melon smell.

❋ Now watermelons are different again. You need to make sure you get it right as they won't ripen any further once they are harvested. Once you notice that it isn't getting any bigger, give it a tap and listen for a dull thud. If it sounds hollow it isn't ready.

   Have a look at the skin. It should be quite dull and have a yellow patch on the bottom. The deeper this colour the more likely it is to be ready, however if it is a little soft to the touch, you may have left it too long.

   Another thing to look for is the curly tendril on the stem where the watermelon stalk meets the vine. Once the melon is ripe this tendril will dry up and turn brown. Provided the rest of the vine isn't brown and shrivelled and dying this is a good indication of ripeness.

LATE SUMMER

By now the novelty of hot sunny days has worn off a little and finding respite from the beating sun is more desirable than basking in it. Tending the garden becomes more pleasurable in the early or late hours of the day. Some crops will be just starting to give you a harvest and others will be coming to an end. You will begin to notice pest and disease increasing in vigour and at this stage it is more of a case of manage not cure. Late summer isn't about a season coming to an end, it is about looking forward. It is a time to prepare for the immediate and long-term future of the garden. There is a constant ebb and flow in the garden and there is always something to do.

Sow

- Outdoors – beans, beetroot, broccoli, Brussels sprouts, cabbage, carrot, cauliflower, celery, leek, lettuce, peas, radish, silverbeet, spinach, spring onion, swede, turnip.

- Succession sow – beetroot, broccoli, carrot, lettuce, radish, spinach and spring onion every 3 weeks or so.

Plant

- Plant seedlings of cabbage, cauliflower, Brussels sprouts, celery, silverbeet, spinach and leek.

Maintain

- Thin carrots.

- Regular deep watering is best.

- Remove weeds while they are small.

- Feed plants weekly or fortnightly with a liquid feed.

- Keep an eye out for pests and disease – be prepared to act quickly!

- Harvest daily.

Harvest

- Beans, beetroot, broccoli, cabbage, carrot, celery, cucumber, eggplant, leek, lettuce, melon, pepper, squash, potato, pumpkin, radish, silverbeet, spinach, spring onion, sweetcorn, tomato and zucchini.

NOTE: This is just a guide – things may happen faster or slower in your garden.

Sweetcorn in the twilight.

IT'S TIME TO THINK ABOUT WINTER GARDENING

Summer's Demise

Now that the peppers are just starting to ripen up, you are up to your ears in tomatoes and have more cucumbers and zucchini than you know what to do with, we need to think about the future.

It is almost too hot to garden right now and stepping out there just to grab a tomato for dinner can cause you to wilt in an instant. But we need to start to plan our winter gardens. It doesn't seem right and it is easy to put things off until it isn't so hot, but the time is right for the cool season crops.

If you act fast you could pop in some more beans, cucumbers and zucchini for a late crop – if the weather holds out and if you need more of these. But for most of our fair weather friends, you will begin to notice from now on that they don't look so perky. The leaves will begin to look tired.

Powdery mildew will be a constant

The garden still has a lot left to give.

battle – if you choose to fight it. You don't really need to as it can be a great handbrake on that exuberant cropping.

Just keep feeding the plants because the soil nutrients will become depleted as we continue to take fruit from the plants. Sometimes nutrient deficiency can look like disease. Disease could be disguised as tired leaves so keep your eyes open so you can notice any dramatic changes. Keep checking the plants for pest and disease as pest numbers will be exponential by now and so infestation of one kind or another almost becomes inevitable.

Eventually the plants will get so tired and the harvest will slow down that it just makes sense to put them out of their misery and pull them out. They can generally go on the compost heap – provided there is no sign of pest or disease. But that is still a way off yet.

But like it or not the garden is in a downward slide. In as little as 6–8 weeks some plants will have given up or been gobbled up and, if the first frost doesn't get there first, the garden will be barren – unless you act now or soon.

Planning Ahead

The winter garden needn't be an empty plot taunting you and collecting weeds. It can still be a productive patch that will provide a fresh crunch alongside the hearty comfort foods. There is lots to choose from, almost

Kohlrabi is a great cool season crop.

have all the room they will need. Especially with root crops as they like to be planted directly into the soil.

You will need to enrich the soil as the summer will have depleted the nutrients. Digging in some organic matter like compost, sheep pellets, blood and bone and or general fertiliser into the immediate area you want to plant in should be enough to give it a boost – you don't need to dig the whole garden over. (Except avoid organic matter for the carrots – they don't like it). It is also ok to continue putting similar winter crops in the same space as the summer ones, but only for this year.

as much as a summer garden. Almost but not quite. But you need to be reminded of lessons from early spring – you may not be able to have it all.

Once you figure out what you want, go back to the spacing chart or look at the instructions on seed packets to see how much room they need. Just to make things interesting, while planning things out you may need to work around existing plants. Having said that most will probably be gone by the time you need the space. This is where interplanting will be useful as you can put small seedlings between the bigger plants and once they are gone the seedlings

Sowing Now

Now it is important to know that while winter crops can grow in cold weather, they really do need the lingering warmth of late summer and early autumn to get them going. This allows them to build up reserves to make them strong seedlings that will get them through harsh winters.

But there are different challenges for seedlings in the late summer compared to spring. The heat is harsh and can dry out seed trays in an hour, so make sure they are kept out of direct sunlight and get enough water that the soil stays consistently moist and doesn't yo-yo between soggy and dry.

You can try overwintering summer plants in a sunny spot indoors over the winter and this will provide a slow, steady taste of summer. It isn't as abundant as in warmer months and if you do try it with a pepper or chilli the heat can be more intense due to the slow growing nature of it – trust me on this one!

TAKE NOTE
WHAT IS GOING ON IN YOUR GARDEN THIS WEEK?

Are you still succession planting summer crops? Which cool season crops will you grow? Are the days still hot? How hot? When was the last time it rained? How are you managing to keep the garden watered?

Putting wet newspaper under the seed tray can be helpful. You have to be particularly vigilant with brassicas. If they dry out as a seedling, it may mean they won't do what they are supposed to when they get bigger and they will bolt straight to seed.

The other problem is pests. Brassica seedlings don't stand a chance against a marauding caterpillar, and a sap-sucking shield beetle will think your tender seedlings are absolutely delicious, so you will need to protect your seedlings with some kind of netting.

Choices

While the glamorous veggies like tomatoes, peppers, chillies and eggplants are mostly summer ones, there is still plenty of choice for the winter garden. Some may be more humble than others, but they all taste good straight from your garden.

Now there is just one other thing to consider with winter growing. Climate.

This is almost more important than the summer garden as how winter behaves in one region is quite different to how it behaves in another. For some gardeners winter is likely to mean snow and for others it stays almost balmy. So the more likely you are to have a snowy winter, the sooner you should put your winter gardens into action.

KNOW YOUR SEEDS

Seeds are the most important part of a vegetable garden and even if you are using seedlings from the garden centre, each plant has been started from a seed. It is easy to take them for granted however the more you understand seeds, the better choices you can make for your garden. They are the lifeblood of a veggie garden.

The first thing you need to know about is what kind of seeds there are out there. This can all be a bit confusing, but it is just like dating and happy families.

Self-pollinating flowers can be pollenated by gently tapping the stem with a buzzing electric toothbrush.

* **Hybrid** – are manually cross-pollinated with other plants in a controlled environment. You can do this yourself if you want.

A hybrid is when you cross two plants with desirable characteristics to make a better plant. They can be chosen because they are the two tastiest plants in a crop, or the ones with the least damage from a disease from the same variety. Or it could be mixing one variety with another and hoping for the best features from both. Normally seeds saved from hybrids don't grow the same as the parent. They are more likely to revert to one of the grandparents or even something completely different.

This is a bit like arranged marriages. The families come together hoping for a good match, but there is no real certainty that the kids from such an arrangement will be so compliant and will often want to find their own way and do their own thing.

F1 is the first generation of a hybrid and an **F2** is the second generation.

* **Open pollinated** is what plants naturally do in nature, and sometimes these can react in the same way a hybrid does with interesting results as there has been no influencing factor in which plants come together.

Harvesting seeds.

This is a bit like free love at a hippy festival. The plants don't really care who pollinates them so long as their seeds are viable. The bees are all over everyone looking for nectar. And the wind blows everything around like hippy music dancing in and out of everyone's heads. Peace out.

✱ **Heirloom or Heritage** are generally original pre-1960 Open Pollinated strains that have over time proven to be quite stable and trusted. They are the ones that sailed the world on settler ships, handed down from generation to generation and between neighbours over back fences.

They are the good kids in the dating world who only stick with the safe parental approved partners.

It doesn't mean they are necessarily the best. Just because they were the best on offer in 1914 doesn't necessarily mean they are best available now. Be open to all types of seeds or you could find yourself limited in flavour or disease resistance among other things.

✱ **Self-pollinating**. These prefer their own company – plants that can pollinate themselves within their own flower. Tomatoes and any members of the Solanaceae family are good at this. So they are pretty good at staying true to their type. Many of these are found as heirloom varieties. Having said that, a pollen laden bee crossing its path or a wind blowing in the right direction can also result in pollination.

✱ **GMO – Genetically Modified Organism**. This is when the genetic makeup of the seed has been changed or modified by molecular techniques in a laboratory. This is a loaded seed in more ways than one. While claiming to benefit the world with more efficient horticultural practices and end world hunger, there are other applications that don't seem as desirable. There is a lot of political and cultural debate about this around the world.

TAKE NOTE
WHAT IS GOING ON IN YOUR GARDEN THIS WEEK?

Have you thought about creating your own special seeds? Do you have any special seeds handed down to you?

_____

_____

_____

_____

_____

_____

_____

_____

SAVING SEEDS

To keep humidity down, add some of those silica gel pouches you get with new handbags, shoes and tortillas into your seed box.

Why you would want to save seeds? Aside from the fun curiosity factor that many gardeners seem to possess 'hmm I wonder what would happen if I do that?', saving seeds will not only save you money, but will over the years create seeds that have been bred by you to suit your specific environmental conditions, climate, pest and disease susceptibility, and match your favourite flavours. Because each garden has its own microclimate and things can be very different to your neighbours so it is great to have seeds perfectly suited to your garden.

How to save seeds

This is a general instruction as there are always seeds with exceptions, so if there is something specific you want to save, do a bit of research for further details.

Ensuring you have the seeds you want to save

Firstly, you can plan ahead to make sure your seeds will be true to type or you can create your own hybrids. Watch the plants in the peak of the season and look for healthy looking specimens. Then get out very early in the morning (preferably a still morning), in time for the flowers to open for the first time and before the bees and other pollinating insects are about. Grab a soft paint brush and take the pollen from one flower – usually a yellow powder and paint it all over the inside centre of another.

Then to make sure the pollinating insects aren't interested in doing the same thing you can either tie a mesh bag over the bloom or remove the petals or both. Once the fruit begins to form then you can remove the mesh bag. It also helps to label

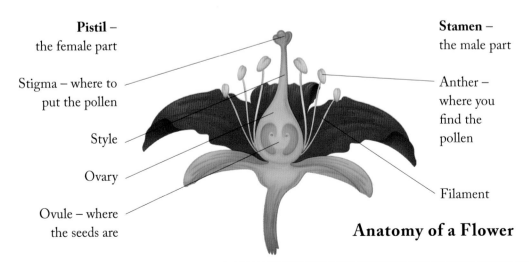

Pistil – the female part

Stigma – where to put the pollen

Style

Ovary

Ovule – where the seeds are

Stamen – the male part

Anther – where you find the pollen

Filament

Anatomy of a Flower

it on the closest branch at this point so you know what you have done and to stop you accidentally eating it.

It is especially import to protect your potential seeds from pollinators if the plant is a tad promiscuous – which is pretty much all open pollinated plants. Pumpkins and the squash family the worst! They will mix it up with whatever is around and so just collecting seeds from a pumpkin is no guarantee you will get the same thing next season – in fact you may get something truly bizarre.

Timing

When it comes to collecting your seeds – it will be in one of two forms – in a dried seed pod like a bean or a pea or embedded in the middle of fleshy fruit like a tomato or cucumber.

You need to make sure that you collect them at the optimum time. If it is in a seed pod, ideally it would be best that it has dried on the plant so it will have reached full maturity. A good way to tell is when seed pods start to open naturally. You may want to bring out the mesh bag again and pop it over almost mature seed pods to ensure you don't lose any that you have taken the effort to pollinate yourself.

Fleshy fruit should also be fully mature on the plant. Tomatoes are easy as this is when they are rosy red ripe and delicious. Peppers need to be red too. Green peppers are just the immature version and so the seeds will not be viable. Green cucumber seeds are also not viable – you need to leave the cucumber on the vine until it goes a dark yellow. Then you can save the seeds.

Zucchinis need to be marrows but they are very promiscuous so if you want the same again – bag that bloom.

Brassicas have a seed pod that will dry out on the plant. Carrots will flower in the second year so you need to leave one or two in the ground and you will be rewarded with hundreds of seeds.

Make sure the seeds come from your healthiest or tastiest plants for the best results.

Collecting and cleaning

* Collect seeds on a dry, sunny day. Avoid seed pods that are damp, as they will rot in storage or may not be ready.
* Bring your seeds inside and spread them out on a paper towel. Leave in a warm dry place with good airflow to ensure they are perfectly dry for storage. Avoid humid locations.
* A good tip is seeds left in their pods will actually keep longer, so it can be much easier and quicker to store them this way. But if you do want to clean them up a little, you can use a sieve and or blow gently to remove the chaff.
* Unless of course it comes in the centre of a fleshy fruit like a tomato. Fleshy seeds are easiest to clean by putting in a sieve under a running tap and rubbing off the pulp until there are only seeds left.
* It is often suggested to put tomato seeds in a jar of water and allow to ferment in order to free the seeds from the gel that surrounds it and it is even alluded to that this will help with viability. However, this isn't essential

and different experts will debate this. I have successfully taken seeds from a yummy tomato in a restaurant – wrapped in a paper napkin and taken it home and stored dry and stuck to the napkin. Then I planted it by chopping off a piece of napkin containing a seed. It worked perfectly well – though I was running the gauntlet not knowing if it was hybrid or not.

In most situations make sure the seeds are completely dry before storing. But remember there are always exceptions so make sure you research things properly first.

Label your seeds

You may know what they are now, but probably won't remember in six months. Try to include as much information as possible – especially if you have attempted your own hybrid cross – you never know you may end up with something really exciting. Date collected, Variety of parent(s) etc.

Storing seeds

This is important for saved and purchased seed.

Please don't store seeds in plastic. They will sweat and rot and be no use to you at all. Avoid keeping them in plastic bags or in plastic containers.

You can buy small wages envelopes which are perfect for storing saved seeds in and you can write all the details on the outside. You can also by glassine bags at craft stores. Glassine is a very thin

and smooth paper that is air and water-resistant, which makes it perfect for storing seeds long term.

The best container to keep your seed collection in is an old-style biscuit tin. This is good for keeping the seeds dry, if it will keep bikkies crisp then it will do the same for your seeds. It is also rodent-proof if you want to keep your seeds in the shed. And it provides a dark environment ideal for long-term storage. The other requirement of seed storage is it needs to be cool.

Some seed storage recommendations suggest storing in the fridge, however if the seed packet is not sealed properly, then you can introduce humidity problems, as the seeds will invariably absorb moisture and encourage mould. Besides I won't have enough room in my fridge for my seed collection.

Others suggest storing seeds in the freezer, however I don't think this is necessary unless you are saving seeds for use when civilisation falls. Moisture can be a problem here, especially if it is a freezer that is opened often. When removing the seed from the freezer there is a risk of the cells in the seed being broken as they defrost and so the seed is no longer viable.

As long as you store your seeds in a cool, dry, dark place where rodents can't get them, then they should be okay to last as long as their general viable period.

How long do seeds last?

Now this is where not all seeds are created equal. Of the common veggies, the longest

Fresh seeds are generally the best seeds to use.

survival period would be about five years but others need to be fresh each season.

An unopened commercial seed packet will be good up until the expiry date and beyond, although the viability will reduce 10% per year after that date. It is a good idea to write the date you opened them on the seed packet.

Below is a handy chart to explain how long seeds should last if they are self-saved or open seed packets – bearing in mind this also depends on correct storage.

YEARS	SEED VIABILITY (If stored correctly)
1	Onion, Parsley, Parsnip
2	Leek, Peppers, Sweetcorn
3	Asparagus, Beans, Broccoli, Carrot, Celery, Peas, Spinach
4	Beetroot, Brussels sprouts, Cabbage, Cauliflower, Eggplant, Melon, Pumpkin, Silverbeet, Squash, Swede, Tomato, Turnip, Zucchini
5	Cucumber, Radish, Lettuce

Testing for viability

You may have a packet open for a while and aren't quite sure if it is worth keeping or throwing away. You don't want to go through the heartbreak and waste of time sowing seeds and waiting for them to come up when it isn't ever going to happen. There is a way to see if the seeds are any good.

* About two to three weeks before you want to sow you seeds, take two or three sheets of paper towel and fold it to the size of a sandwich-style snap-lock type of plastic bag.

* Label the plastic bag with the name of the seed and the date you started this process.
* Moisten the paper towel under the tap, but not so it is wringing wet.
* Place ten seeds evenly on the paper towel.
* Gently slide the paper towel and the seeds into the plastic bag. You can either leave the bag open to give good airflow or inflate the bag with a straw and seal it.
* Then place it in a warm, dark place like a hot water cupboard.
* Check on it daily.
* After ten days you should be able to roughly figure out the percentage of viable seeds. Unless it is something you really want to grow I personally wouldn't bother below seven out of ten seeds germinated. If it is something you really want to grow, then use lots of seeds and hope for the best.

TAKE NOTE
WHAT IS GOING ON IN YOUR GARDEN THIS WEEK?

How many seeds packets do you have? How are you storing them? Where are you keeping them? Have you tested the viability of your old seeds? How did you get on?

THE INS AND OUTS OF COMPOST

Wandering around any garden centre and you will see bags and bags of compost available for the keen gardener to enrich their soil. It is such a fabulous product to improve the quality of your soil that you couldn't possibly use too much.

Compost will improve the soil structure, help with the retention of moisture, slowly release nutrients into the soil to be made available for growing plants, increase the quantity and quality of the harvest, feed the soil organisms and attract earthworms. It can even improve the health and disease resistance of the plants.

When you are starting out, it is perfectly fine to buy in bags or even pick up a trailer-load or two. However, adding compost to the garden isn't something you do once when you first create your garden. Healthy gardens benefit from compost being added regularly to replenish the soil and replace what was used by the plants of the previous season. Active gardens that don't get fed can eventually starve and will produce poor-quality plants. You need to put back what has been taken and long term this can get a little expensive.

The good news is compost is quite easy to make and it makes perfect sense to use the waste products from your garden to replenish the soil in the future. By making your own you have control over what has been added to it and how it has been treated. With many crops, you only actually eat a small proportion of the plant and the rest can be composted and as the season comes to an end you will be generating quite a lot of garden waste.

There are a few rules about making compost, but once you get these sorted you will be well on your way to be creating your own great soil conditioner.

Avoid using compost that is warm or doesn't smell good. Generally, this means it isn't ready yet. Finished compost has a rich crumbly soil-like feel and should smell quite earthy and you shouldn't be able to recognise its original ingredients.

Good compost should have a mix of greens and browns.

Three bin compost system.

Ideally you should have a 2:1 blend of brown and green material. This gives the perfect balance for the micro-organisms to get to work and break it all down. If you have too much carbon your pile will take ages to rot. If you have too much nitrogen in your pile, there is a high chance it will become quite stinky.

Brown materials are carbon-rich and include:

- Straw
- Dry leaves
- Twigs
- Dry corn stalks
- Cardboard
- Sawdust
- Shredded paper
- Wood chips

Green materials are nitrogen-rich and include:

- Vegetable scraps
- Coffee grounds
- General garden waste
- Young weeds
- Grass clippings
- Pruning waste
- Seaweed
- Well-rotted vegetarian and chicken manure

Don't add these to your compost pile:

- Meat and dairy products
- Cooked food
- Fats and oils
- Brightly printed papers
- Diseased plant materials
- Manure from meat-eating creatures
- Plants covered in pests
- Weed seeds and weeds that don't seem to want to die.

Home compost systems generally don't get hot enough to destroy pests, disease, seeds and stubborn weeds. Anything not suitable for putting in the compost should be put out with the rubbish or burnt. Adding cooked foods can attract rats and no one wants that. Manure from cats, dogs and even people can introduce diseases that the gardener can contract and so it is important to avoid these, especially in an edible garden.

Even a pile at the far end of the garden will eventually rot down and give you compost, however there are many options available to speed up the process. Turning the pile at least monthly will aerate the compost and hurry things along. There are two main processes – hot composting and cold composting.

Hot composting is when the blend of brown and green material and moisture levels are perfect and the temperature rises rapidly as the microorganisms get on with the job of breaking down the material. Turning the pile often will increase the speed of the process. It could take as little as several weeks or up to several months. It takes considerable effort to manage this process, but is worth it in the long run.

Cold composting is pretty much just letting things get on with the rotting process in their own time. It can up to a year or two to see the end product.

You could also try:

* **Closed bins** – these look like a black figure lurking at the back of your garden cold processing your compost. They are great for small spaces, however the yield is smaller due to the size of the bin and takes a little longer to create compost.
* **Pit Composting** – which is basically a hole in the ground where you toss everything compostable. It can take six months to a year, and is more suited to long-term enriching of the soil in situ.
* **Open bins** – This can be as simple as some chicken wire wrapped around some stakes, some old pallets tied together or an elaborate structure built from timber. This can be used for hot or cold composting, depending how much effort you want to give it.
* **Tumbler** – this is a drum shaped system, where you load it up and give it a turn every time you wander past. This produces compost faster than a compost pile as the contents are being aerated each time it is turned. Although due to the size of the bin the batches are small.

Worms for the farm.

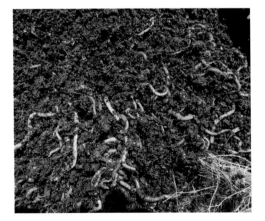

TAKE NOTE

WHAT IS GOING ON IN YOUR GARDEN THIS WEEK?

How is the weather in the garden? Is it beginning to cool down yet? How are your summer crops faring? What are your worst pests and diseases this season?

....

....

....

....

....

....

....

....

....

....

Whatever way you choose to compost your garden waste – before long you will be able to create your own compost to reinvigorate your soil every season and save you a bit of money too!

TAKE CARE: *using composts and potting mixes as there is always a risk of Legionnaires' disease. It comes from a naturally occurring soil borne bacteria that can be inhaled if the soil or compost you are working with is particularly dusty. It is a good idea to wear gloves while working in the garden and wear a mask if there is a risk of breathing in soil particles or you are working in dusty conditions.*

FARMING WORMS

Make sure your worm farm is made of material that excludes the like as the worms are sensitive to bright light.

You may not have a very big garden, but you can still get involved with large scale farming. Worm farming.

Having a worm farm can provide you with rich worm castings (poop) and worm tea (wees) that will enrich the quality of your soil and make nutrients easily accessible to your plants. Farming worms can add a lot of value to your garden, but any old worm won't do, you need specialist compost worms. They are different from the earthworms you find in your garden. Earthworms like to live deep in the soil where they eat organic matter in the soil and their tunnels aerate the soil and their castings enrich the soil. Compost worms live in the surface layer of the soil and eat the plant material that is rotting there.

By using these composting worms, you can concentrate their efforts into making them create their rich by-products that you can use wherever you want to in your garden. You can get your hands on the right kind of worms from a generous friend willing to share some from their healthy worm farm, or by purchasing them from a local supplier.

You also need somewhere for them to live and can either buy a farm or make one. The basic design of a worm farm is a generally a multi-layered structure. The top level is where the food is kept and where the worms will come to eat. The middle layer is where the worms live when they aren't eating. They are a little messy in that they poop in their living environment, however the farm is set up so the liquid waste falls through to the lower level where this nutrient-rich material is available for collection. There should be a tap to make collection simple. Once you have drained it off dilute it with 1 part worm wee to seven parts water for a rich plant fertiliser.

Castings take longer to develop and accumulate where the worms live. To gather these, push aside the top layers of bedding and you should find what looks like rich dark soil. This is the Black Gold you can use to enrich your soil and feed your plants, help to improve the general health of your garden.

TAKE NOTE
WHAT IS GOING ON IN YOUR GARDEN THIS WEEK?

How are your cool season seedlings doing?
When was the last time you had rain?
Are you staying on top the weeds?

EARLY AUTUMN

Summer often slips into autumn unnoticed and without much fanfare. There is a reluctance to allow a great growing season to come to an end. The continued warm weather allows the gardener to carry on often under the guise of an Indian Summer. But as the days begin to noticeably shorten, the mornings start with a chill in them and the leaves on the trees age gracefully with a golden hue, there is no getting away from it, the start of autumn heralds the beginning of the end for the productive summer garden.

Sow

- Outdoors – beetroot, broad beans, broccoli, Brussels sprouts, cabbage, carrot, cauliflower, leek, lettuce, spinach, onion, spring onion, peas, radish, silverbeet, spinach, swede and turnip.

Plant

- Plant seedlings of beetroot, broccoli, Brussels sprouts, cauliflower, spinach silverbeet, and leek.

Maintain

- Sow a green manure cover crop.

- As crops finish, test the soil to see how best to re-enrich it.

- Thin carrots.

- Remove spent plants and add to compost.

- Regular deep watering is best.

- Remove weeds while they are small.

- Feed plants weekly or fortnightly with a liquid feed.

- Keep an eye out for pests and disease.

- Harvest regularly.

Harvest

- Beans, beetroot, broccoli, Brussels sprouts, cabbage, carrot, cauliflower, celery, eggplant, leek, melon, peas, pepper, pumpkin, radish, silverbeet, spinach, spring onion, squash, sweetcorn, tomato and zucchini.

NOTE: This is just a guide – things may happen faster or slower in your garden.

Chillies ripen as the heat ebbs away.

HOW TO KNOW WHEN PUMPKINS ARE READY

One of the iconic vegetables of autumn has to be the pumpkin and whether is to be carved and lit up with lights to decorate a front step or carefully stored in a cool, dry, dark shed for a comforting midwinter soup or stew, it is one of the last vegetables to be harvested from the summer garden and its removal often marks the end of a productive growing season.

If you are growing these wonderful vegetables then by now you should have pumpkin vines scrambling all over your garden, threatening to take over. Amongst the large leaves should be some large treasures.

However, for the keen gardener there is often a temptation to harvest too soon, before the flesh has a chance to develop its sweet, rich flavours and the wonderful keeping properties that allow it to store well into the winter to mature. A pumpkin harvested at the peak ripeness and treated correctly should store for five months so it is important to get it right.

Signs that your pumpkin may be ready to harvest:
※ The leaves all around it will begin to die off and go a bit brown and crispy.
※ The stem should be hard and 'corky' in appearance and more brown than green.
※ Give the pumpkin a tap. It should sound hollow.
※ Push the skin with your fingernail. It should be thick and strong enough to not be marked. If your nail manages to pierce the skin, then it is still not ready and try again in a few days.

The exception to all of this is if the weatherman says there is going to be

Are they ready or not?

Don't carry the pumpkin by the stalk in case it snaps off. It isn't a handle.

a heavy frost, then race outside and harvest them all. Pumpkins can tolerate a light frost but a heavy one will ruin them.

preferably up off the ground and not touching each other.

✳ Come winter all you need to do is decide how you want to eat your delicious pumpkin.

How to harvest pumpkin:
If you get this wrong, they may rot while in storage and no one wants that.

✳ Take a sharp knife or secateurs and cut the stalk as close to the vine as possible. It is important to have a long stalk so it can dry off, seal the pumpkin and protect it from rot.

Prepare pumpkins for storage:
Check the pumpkin over and make sure there is no bruising or damage. If there is then you may need to eat it sooner rather than later.

✳ Prepare a dilute bleach solution of 1 part bleach, 9 parts water and give the pumpkins a good wash to remove any pests and disease lurking on the surface that could rot the pumpkin in storage. Then dry it well.

✳ Leave the pumpkins in a dry sunny place, like a windowsill or greenhouse for two weeks. Then turn them over and leave them for another two weeks. This cures the pumpkin and makes sure the skins are nice and hard and any that may not have been perfectly ripe will get there during curing. It will also sweeten up the flesh and make them even more delicious.

✳ Finally store them in cool, dark place with plenty of airflow around them –

TAKE NOTE
WHAT IS GOING ON IN YOUR GARDEN THIS WEEK?

Have you noticed the days getting shorter? Which crops are coming to an end? What are you still harvesting?

....

....

....

....

....

....

....

....

....

....

....

....

....

HOW DID YOUR SEASON GO?

As you stand in your fading garden, you should feel proud in all that you have achieved. After months and months of effort you have made it through the craziest growing season and will have been rewarded with the fruits of your labour. But you have gained something more valuable than the glorious taste of fresh tomatoes or the reward of what is effectively free food, and the blessing of being able to share your bounty with your friends and family.

The most important thing you have reaped from your garden is experience. You now know how things grow and what they need. You will probably know what a thirsty plant looks like and you may even know what disastrous damage some pests can do. It is one thing to read about these things, but to actually experience it and understand how a plant will react to various situations they face during the growing season in your garden in priceless.

Throughout the growing season you should have been taking notes along the way as to how things have been going and what you have been doing. This information is more like a snapshot of what going on at the time, a record of events and observations and very useful.

Take notes while it is still fresh in your mind.

Was your irrigation system adequate?

Did your structures hold up?

A gardener is always learning, and if you take some time to analyse the season your garden will show you how you can be a better gardener.

Now, in your fading garden, is a good time to look over those notes, and look over your garden and look at it in a big picture way. Ask yourself, now that you know what you know, is there anything you would do differently?

❋ Is your garden in the right place?

❋ Is your garden big enough?

❋ Did you enjoy what you grew?

❋ Did you grow enough or even too much?

❋ Did you give things enough room or do you need to space them further apart next time?

❋ Was keeping the garden watered easy or a bit of challenge?

❋ Would you make stakes taller or stronger?

By taking the time to review the season and asking yourself these questions and any others that come to mind will ensure you have a better garden next season and in the many seasons to come.

Often in the heady days of spring, it is easy to get carried away and end up repeating the long forgotten mistakes of last season.

TAKE NOTE
WHAT IS GOING ON IN YOUR GARDEN THIS WEEK?

How well do you think your growing season went? Is there anything you would do differently? Has anything surprised you with how well or how badly it went?

....

....

....

....

....

....

....

....

....

....

RELUCTANTLY CLEARING AWAY THE CROPS

Take photos of the root structure or the way the stem has grown if it will help you remember.

As the weeks progress deeper into autumn the garden reaches a point where the inevitable happens and you need to pull out the plants. Most of the plants in the vegetable garden are grown as annuals and like all good things, their productive life comes to an end.

Even in this sad moment as you say goodbye to the season take a moment to have a good look at the dead plants. There is much for the keen gardener to learn, even from the dead and dying.

Look at its growth habit:
* How tall was it?
* Did it branch out?
* How strong were the branches?
* Did it need support?
* Was the support you provided strong enough?

Look at the roots:
Was it a shallow rooting structure or did the roots go down deep?
* Was it a mass of roots or just one tap root?
* Can you find the nodules on the beans and pea roots?

By examining the plant, you can get a better understanding of how the plant grows and so next season you can make sure you allow for this when preparing your

Remove all traces of the plant, any fallen fruit or buried root as they have the potential to harbour pest and disease in your garden.

garden. For example, if the roots are deep, then make sure you enrich your soil with compost and fertilisers to a deeper depth. Or if the roots are shallow, you may want to water the plants deep and less frequently to encourage the roots to grow a little deeper.

Knowing how zucchini grow will help next season.

Or maybe you have realised that things were possibly planted a little too close together, especially with plants like the peppers where the branches are quite fragile and can be easily snapped while looking for ripe ones. Or if the zucchini sprawled off, all over the other plants. Looking at its carcass can help you to understand its growth habit and make it easier for you to plant it in the right place next season.

Once you have examined them, most plants are perfectly ok to put on the compost heap, but check for pest and disease first. If in doubt, throw it out.

TAKE NOTE
WHAT IS GOING ON IN YOUR GARDEN THIS WEEK?

What did you observe as you looked at your dead plants that will help you next season? How cold is it getting overnight?

....

....

....

....

....

....

....

Sweetcorn roots anchor this tall plant.

Another load for the compost.

PUTTING THE GARDEN TO BED

Sheet mulching.

As the summer garden comes to an end and you seem to have more bare earth than lush productive growth, you need to decide what you want to do with the garden. You can't just leave it as nature hates bare earth and will try to cover it over and before you know it you will find your garden full of weeds.

It can be tempting to just leave the garden as is with its dead and dying plants still tied to the stake and the last of the fruit still clinging to the plant in various stages of decay, thinking you'll sort it out in the spring. This isn't such a good idea as the weeds will grow up through it, pest and disease will find a wonderful place to spend the winter and it will be much harder to sort it out in the spring.

A plan of action is needed and it depends on what you want to do with your garden over the winter months.

If you want to keep growing food, then keep planting things now. In the chill of winter things grow much slower so depending on where you live you may not see a harvest until it starts to warm up again in the spring, but it will be better than not having planted anything at all. Or you could find yourself in a milder winter and will be able to harvest something to eat throughout the cool season. There are many choices for plants that tolerate the cool weather – or even prefer it, so check out what is suited to growing in your specific climate for the best results.

You may decide you don't want to do anything at all, but you still need to protect the soil from the weeds.

Sowing a cover crop.

Add manure to the garden.

* You can do this by popping down a sheet mulch. This is a thick layer of material that weeds find it difficult to grow in.
* You could spread a thick layer of manure or compost so the worms will do the work of dragging it deep into the soil into the root zone over the winter.
* You could lay some cardboard over the garden – but avoid the shiny printed kind as the inks generally aren't garden friendly and the shine often comes from a thin layer of plastic. If you find this is a bit unsightly then you could cover it with a layer of your favourite mulch.
* Or you could plant a cover crop to grow a green manure, which will re-enrich the soil, keep the weeds at bay with its presence and give you something nice and green to look at over the winter.

Covering the ground with plastic may seem like a good idea, however it doesn't allow the ground to breathe and the rain can't get in and so the soil can become what is known as sour and is quite unhealthy.

MID AUTUMN

Most of the summer garden has been cleared away and its fresh tastes are just a fond memory. The nights are really beginning to close in now and waking up to darkness is something you are getting used to. The temperatures are still falling and has you reaching for thick socks and a jumper, but it is still not quite beanie and scarf weather yet. Autumn is a gentle season and eases us into the chilly season ever so gently. The first frost of the season isn't too far away and the anticipation of it keeps the gardener on their toes.

Sow	*Plant*	*Maintain*	*Harvest*
• Outdoors – broadbean, cabbage, carrot, leek, lettuce, onion, spring onion, peas, radish, silverbeet, spinach, swede and turnip	• Transplant seedlings of broccoli, Brussels sprouts, cabbage, cauliflower, celery, leek, lettuce, silverbeet and spinach. • Plant onion sets. • Plant strawberries.	• Earth up leeks. • Sow a green manure cover crop. • As crops finish, test the soil to see how best to re-enrich it. • Thin carrots. • Remove spent plants and add to compost • Remove weeds while they are small.	• Beetroot, broccoli, Brussels sprouts, cabbage, carrot, cauliflower, celery, leek, parsnip, peas, pepper, pumpkin, radish, silverbeet, spinach, spring onion, swede and turnip. NOTE: This is just a guide – things may happen faster or slower in your garden.

Autumn hosts such rich colours.

COVER CROPS

It is important not to let your cover crop go to seed or you will invite a lot of potential weeds into your garden for quite some time.

The decision to grow cover crops is a great way to keep the garden alive over the winter months. Sown now in the lingering warmth of autumn they can bring so much value to the productivity in the garden come spring.

The basic premise of a cover crop is to sow beneficial crops now that grow slowly over the winter months. Then about six to eight weeks before the last frost of spring,

Lupin makes a great cover crop.

or just as the crop flowers while the stems are still tender and not yet woody, which is most cases is around a similar time, the crop is dug into the soil where it rots down and adds organic matter into the soil. This improves the structure, feeds the worms, improves the microbial life and provides nutrients for the new plants.

There are various crops suitable to be used as a green manure.

Legumes
These are the most common type of cover crop. These are the lupins, broad beans, field beans, lucerne and even clover. The advantage of these plants is they have the nodules on their roots that fix nitrogen from the soil and convert it to a form easily accessed by plants. A crop like is great to plant after or before one that is considered a gross feeder or used a lot of nutrients

Sow your cover crop thickly.

from the soil by growing rather large, like sweetcorn, or one that created a lot of foliage like your leafy greens.

Mustard
Another common cover crop and it is said to have healing properties that can cleanse the soil. This can come in quite handy if you have had problems with soil pests or disease over the growing season. However,

Dig your cover crop in before it flowers.

it isn't recommended for sowing before or after brassicas as they are in the same family and are a risk factor for a disease called club root, which if you find it in your garden it is very difficult to remove and you may never be able to grow brassicas there again.

Grain crops

These are also great cover crops as when dug back into the soil they add structure. However instead of digging them in you can harvest them, dry them off and use them as a mulch on top of the garden around your new season seedlings to retain moisture and reduce weeds.

There are other plants suitable for use as a cover crop, the main quality would be to be tolerant of frost and could cope with the cold, wet weather winter tends to throw at the garden. There will be something out there suitable for your specific climate.

Digging in the cover crop sounds a lot easier than done. The easiest way seems to be:

1. To pull up the plants and break or chop them into short lengths and set aside.

2. Dig a trench in the garden to about a spades depth – roughly about the depth of the root zone of the plants you are going to grow.
3. Add the chopped up material to the trench and cover over.
4. Repeat until you end up with the organic material roughly distributed throughout your garden. Leave for it to break down.
5. By the time you are ready to start your garden you should have a lovely rich layer to be mixed into the soil as part of the important foundation of having a healthy soil in order to have a healthy garden.

HYGIENE IN THE GARDEN

Plastic pots are a little better than the traditional terracotta pots as they can be quite porous and harder to clean properly.

In the dirty world of gardening it can be surprising to realise hygiene is actually very important to the health and well-being of your garden. There are a few things you can do to make sure your garden is in tip top condition so you can have the very best quality vegetables to eat.

Early in the season

❋ Caring for your seedlings and container plants is important as they are probably the most vulnerable to a sad demise for a number of reasons. You can reduce the risk of pest and disease by using potting mixes, seed-raising mixes, fertilisers and anything else you are likely to add to the container from reputable suppliers. It isn't worth their reputation to sell you something that is likely to harm your plants.

❋ Pots and containers don't need to be specific for the garden and you are only really limited by your creativity and what you can find to upcycle. Whatever you do choose to use, make sure it is clean before you start. It also pays to give it a wash once you've finished with it and store them away clean for re-use next season. Give them a good scrub to remove all trace of dirt and debris, then soak in a 10% bleach solution. Allow to air dry.

During the season

If you get a diseased plant and you've tried to fix it but it doesn't seem to be working, it can be best to cut your losses and rip it out. It may be disappointing to lose one tomato plant, but to lose them all would be devastating. And bin it or burn it, but don't put it on the compost pile.

❋ Gather up any fallen leaves and fruit regularly to reduce the chance of any pests or disease making themselves at home in the soil and also removing potential hiding places for the unwanted, like slugs and snails and other nasties.

❋ Take care of any damaged plants straight away as this can become an open door to a whole raft of unwanted pests and disease.

❋ Keep your tools clean and put them away after using them. You may

Make sure the pots you use are very clean.

consider painting bright colours on the handles so you can find them easily after a hard day in the garden.

❋ Keeping tools clean is even more important if you have been working on diseased plants. You should clean them between plants to avoid the spread of disease. In this situation you can use a 10% bleach solution.

After using your tools, plunge them into a bucket of sand with about 500ml of mineral oil mixed in. This will help keep them clean and sharp. Keep this bucket inside the door to your shed for easy access.

TAKE NOTE

WHAT IS GOING ON IN YOUR GARDEN THIS WEEK?

What plans do you need to put in place to ensure your garden stays clean and tidy all season long?

....

....

....

....

....

....

....

....

At the end of the season

❋ When you clear the garden, any structures, labels, stakes and poles that you are likely to use again should also be given a thorough clean in the same way as the pots. Check for any pests that may be hiding, especially in the centre of bamboo stakes.

❋ If you have a greenhouse, now is a great time to give it a thorough scrub down and disinfect. Make sure you pay good attention to all areas including the walls, floors and shelving.

❋ Have a bit of a spring clean to clear up any rubbish that may have found its way into your garden.

Empty out your greenhouse and give it a good scrub.

GARDEN TOOLS

If push came to shove you could grow things in your garden by using just your bare hands, but it would be hard work and fortunately there arc lots of tools out there that do different jobs to make life easy for the gardener.

Standing in the tool section of a garden centre can be quite overwhelming as there seems to be so many variations of each tool. Then there are the specialist ones that are for the one task that only gets done once a year. There are also many cool gadgets and tempting things that promise to improve the way things are done but it you are honest with yourself they aren't really necessary.

Tools that have some kind of sharp cutting edge, like a spade, hoe or secateurs, can quickly become dull with use. Check your tools often and re-sharpen with a whetstone, file or grinder to ensure the task at hand requires the least amount of effort possible.

The tools that could almost be called essential for the keen gardener, although 'most useful' is probably a better description, are:

1. **Spade** – Not to be mistaken for a shovel, this is used for cutting to the soil and digging. It is the tool of choice for early season preparing of the soil. It makes a great job of turning over the earth. You will use your spade a lot so make sure you buy one that is a good length and weight so you can use it comfortably.

2. **Fork** – this a really handy tool to have and can be used to loosen soil, turn in compost and fertilisers and prise roots from the ground. These also come in different sizes and even different shapes for different purposes so find one that suits you best.

3. **Trowel** – this is a small hand tool and perfect for digging holes to plant seedlings into. Some even come with a ruler etched into them so you know just how deep your hole is.

4. **Secateurs** – There are so many different kinds and they are an important tool for pruning trees and shrubs. However, in the vegetable garden you just need a sturdy pair with a sharp blade for help removing wayward branches, cutting out tomato laterals, harvesting produce without damaging the plant and many other uses.

5. **Shovel** – This is a great tool for scooping up and moving large amounts of material like getting compost or

Buy the best tools you can afford.

mulch onto a garden bed. A spade could do the job, but a shovel will get through the chore much quicker and easier.

6. **Rake** – This has a few uses in the garden. Raking over the soil can remove sticks and stones and create a fine tilth that makes the soil perfect for sowing seeds into. It can also help bring together for easy collection fallen leaves or weeds that may have been overenthusiastically pulled out and left on the side of the garden.

7. **Wheelbarrow** – not entirely necessary but great to carry heavy things around the garden. You can also get trolleys that do the same job but may be easier to manoeuvre than the one-wheeled wheelbarrow.

8. **Hoe** – pushing a hoe up and down the rows regularly can help keep the weeds down around your plants and stop sun-baked soil from forming a hard crust that may resist absorbing water. Keeping it sharp will make the task easier but don't go too close to your plants or you may end up damaging them or at worst, decapitating them.

9. **Gloves** – Many gardeners like to feel the soil between their fingers and bear the mark of a gardener with their chipped nails and dirt-stained hands. Others like to protect their hands with gloves. Sometimes gloves are needed as there are tasks just too nasty for even the hardiest 'free' gardener. There are many kinds out there, so make sure they fit well and breathe or things can get a bit whiffy at the end of a hard day in the garden.

10. **Hose** – spend as much as you can afford when buying a hose as the cheaper ones tend to kink easily which is very annoying and also perish within a season or two. Some hoses also claim to be safe for drinking and won't leach harsh chemicals onto your edible plants. Also make sure your hose is long enough to reach from your tap to the far reaches of the garden to make things easy for you.

11. **Nozzle** – Holding your thumb across the end of the hose is a simple way of squirting water around the garden but it isn't efficient or sustainable. A nozzle connected to the end will do a much better job and there are many kinds available from the simple spray of varying strengths to a fancy nozzle with half a dozen ways of delivering water from a gentle mist suitable for seeds to a jet that will power wash the side of your house!

12. **Watering can** – While a hose will do most of your watering jobs, a watering can is useful for small jobs, watering plants the hose can't reach, applying fertilizers or gently watering seedlings in a greenhouse.

13. **Bucket** – a completely indispensable item. In fact, you should have several of them. They are good for popping weeds into as you work your way across the garden, mixing up fertilizers, carrying small tools about the garden, lugging water. Even holes poked in the bottom turn them into affordable planters if you run out of room in the bed. The uses for a bucket will surprise you.

It doesn't take long to find your favourite tools.

14. **Scissors** – These are quite handy to have available in the garden, from harvesting herbs and other produce to cutting string, opening seed packets and bags of compost.

15. **Stylish basket** – this is for harvesting your veggies into. After all the effort you have taken to grow your harvest, it wouldn't seem right to just shove them into a bucket or plastic bag. You want it to look lovely and then everyone will admire all you have achieved.

Wiping over the wooden handles of your tools with linseed oil will help prevent the wood from drying out, causing splinters and will help make them last longer.

LEAF MOULD

Take care if you collect leaves from a roadside as it may have litter or gifts from passing dogs and if it is a particularly busy street then there may be a degree of exhaust pollution.

Here in the heart of autumn the trees around us are doing what deciduous trees do and giving us a magnificent display of golden-hued leaves and then as they transition from green to rich, deep yellows and reds, they finally turn brown and slip from the tree and fall to the ground.

Many people see this annual inundation as a problem that needs to be raked up and hauled away. As a gardener this is like a gift from the sky, not to be raked up and thrown away, but raked up and treasured as this is the source of the most incredible soil conditioner.

The easiest way to deal with autumn leaves is to sweep them up onto the garden as a mulch, to suppress weeds over the winter months. Although this does come with a drawback, as slugs and snails love to hide amongst the many layers of the leaves.

Instead of sweeping them up, try running over them with your lawn mower with the catcher on. This serves two purposes: (1) it picks them all up; and (2) it chops them up a little to help speed up the process of breaking down into leaf mould.

This is a wonderful thing for the garden

Set the leaves aside and then wait.

Leaves from the gutter may have hidden dangers.

How can you source large amounts of
leaves? Have you had much rain? How are
your cool season crops doing? What are you
harvesting?

however, it isn't as nutritious as compost
but it is a great soil conditioner that helps
to develop soil structure, improves moisture
retention in the soil and the worms love it.

To turn the leaves to leaf mould is a
simple process but it does take a while.

1. Fill a large black plastic garden bag
   with leaves and moisten with water, so
   it won't dry out.
2. Use your garden fork to poke some
   holes to allow air into the bag.
3. Tie it up and put it in an out of the
   way place and leave.

*If you want to collect
leaves from public places
or beneath trees you don't own,
make sure you are allowed. You may
look a little odd to the non-gardener
while you are out there gathering
leaves, but you wouldn't want to
get into trouble for it too.*

4. Check occasionally and if it gets a bit
   dry add a splash more water.

Or instead of hiding it away in black plastic
bags you can use chicken wire to make a
column about a metre high and fill it with
leaves. You will still need to keep it damp,
but not soggy so you may need a lid to
protect it from the rain.

Whichever method you chose it should
take 6–12 months to achieve a lovely rich
leaf mould from the autumn leaves. It is
a great soil conditioner as the leaves are
rich in carbon, which is why it would take
longer to break down than the blend of
materials normally added to your compost.

If you make this an annual autumn
activity, then you will end up continuous
supply of great leaf mould to improve the
soil in your garden.

LATE AUTUMN

The shorter days leave us with no doubt that this is the last stop before winter. Life in the garden has pretty much slowed down to match the waning desire to get out there in the increasingly chilly weather. Yet for the keen gardener there are the last few tidying chores, and a few late sneaky plantings and general pottering about that can fill the few opportunities when the sun still shines brightly and brings a gentle warmth to the otherwise dull days.

Sow	*Plant*	*Maintain*	*Harvest*
• Outdoors – broadbean, cabbage, onion, spring onion, peas, radish and spinach	• Plant seedlings of broccoli, cabbage, cauliflower, lettuce, silverbeet, spinach and spring onions.	• Earth up celery and leeks.	• Beetroot, broccoli, Brussels sprouts, cabbage, carrot, cauliflower, celery, leek, parsnip, peas, radish, silverbeet, spinach, spring onion, swede and turnip.
NOTE: This is just a guide – things may happen faster or slower in your garden.	• Plant garlic, shallots and onion sets. • Plant strawberries.	• Thin carrots and other autumn sown crops. • Cut back asparagus when stems turn yellow and apply compost.	

Misty foggy days.

FROSTY NIGHTS

Not many plants can withstand a good frost.

If it hasn't happened already, it is only matter of time before that first frost hits and if you have plants in the garden then you want to be ready for it, to protect them from the worst of it, but also to extend your growing season for as long as possible.

Some plants don't mind the cold and will stand out there all winter long whatever the weather throws at it. Others are a little more sensitive and will curl up their toes if it gets too cold. The rate of growth slows right down and in some cases completely stops until things warm up again.

Frost can cause a lot of damage to tender plants taken by surprise. It isn't so much the freezing of the liquid within the plant that causes harm, but the defrosting damages the cell walls and complex structure that holds the plant together begins to break down. Plants hit by frost are generally limp, quickly go brown or black and really don't look good.

Frost cloth, bed sheets, newspaper or any similar material thrown over a plant at night before a frost is due to hit can protect plants from harm. Once the sun comes up remove the frost cover so your plants can continue to grow with good airflow. At this time of year, it is important to watch the weather forecast.

You can reduce the risk of frost damage by:
* Planting your cool season crops in sheltered locations in your gardens.
* Avoid planting in places that are more likely than others to see any frost or are the last parts of the garden to defrost during the winter months.
* Avoid feeding plants with fertilizers that will encourage new growth as these tender shoots are most at risk of frost damage.
* Most plants hate wet feet and even more so when there is freezing water swilling about their roots, so make sure your garden is free draining.
* You can keep those roots warm by applying a mulch and this will help keep the soil from freezing.
* Planting things in containers is a good idea if you get a lot of hard frosts as you can move the plants out of harm's way when a frost is predicted.

> *If your plants do get hit by frost, remember most of the damage is in the defrosting so if you leap out of bed before the sun reaches the garden and hose off the ice and allow your plant to defrost slowly you should reduce the chance of devastating damage.*

Soil can benefit from being frozen.

FROST ISN'T ALL BAD

Aside from harming your tender plants, frost actually has benefits for your garden and the arrival overnight of a hard frost is actually cause for celebration.

It can save your back a little in the spring. When the moisture in the soil freezes, it expands and breaks up any clumps in the soil and improves the soil structure. So if your soil is particularly hard and full of lumps but possibly a little dry, race out there with a hose and dampen it down if a frost is forecast and your soil will become a little crumblier with each freezing night.

The freezing temperatures can also help control pests and disease. It disrupts life cycles, destroys fungal spores and bacteria, freezes insect eggs and overwintering pests and even damages weed seeds. It isn't a great cure all, but knocks the populations of these undesirables back so you have a bit of a head start to the new season.

The other advantage of frost is it can sweeten many crops including the brassicas, leeks and parsnip. In normal circumstances the plants create energy as sugar from the sun in the leaves and store it as starch. However, when the plant senses a frost is coming it converts the starch back into sugar and sends it into all the cells to act as a kind of antifreeze. The result is great for the gardener as this sugar makes things taste so much better.

TAKE NOTE
WHAT IS GOING ON IN YOUR GARDEN THIS WEEK?

Have you seen the first frost yet? Are you ready for it? Where is your preferred place to find out the weather forecast?

ONIONS AND GARLIC

Grow onions from sets.

Onions

There are several varieties of onions available and they generally fall into three groups: early, mid and late season. The earlies benefit from being started in the lingering warmth of autumn, the mid seasons like to be sown in the freezing depths of winter and the late ones can go in anytime from mid autumn to late winter. If the wrong variety gets planted at the wrong time they can bolt to seed.

So the old wives' tale advising planting on the shortest day so you can harvest on the longest is really just a guide as it's not the only day you can grow onions, there is a window of several months.

Onions are hungry plants and need a well-prepared rich soil to spend the season in. When growing from seed you can start them off indoors in seed trays and transplant them when they are about 15cm tall. You can also start onions from sets, which are immature bulbs that have been harvested and cured the season before and will continue growing once you plant them out.

Remove any flower stems as they emerge as they divert energy from the growing bulbs.

The bulb grows mostly above the surface of the soil so it is important not to plant them too deep – just enough to cover the roots is good enough.

During the growing period, make sure the soil stays moist but not soggy wet and you can give them a feed once the bulbs start to form. Keep the garden weed free because they really hate the competition.

They can take six months or so to be ready to harvest. You can tell when this is as the tops begin to fall over. When you harvest them, leave them in the sun for a few days for the papery skins to dry out to protect the onion for storage.

Garlic

This is such a versatile vegetable and ends up in almost every meal. The good news is it couldn't be easier to grow.

The old adage "plant on the shortest day, and harvest it on the longest" is often applied to garlic too, but what garlic basically needs a period of chill to stimulate the leaf growth and then as the day lengthens and things warm up it switches over to making those bulbs nice and fat. So they can be planted once it starts to get cold in autumn until early spring while it is still cold.

Garlic is one of the very hungry crops, so you need to prepare your soil well and make sure it is jam-packed with compost, rich organic material, well-rotted manure and any other amendments you like to add. You can also feed the crop throughout the growing season to encourage bigger bulbs.

Once your soil is sorted you can plant the garlic. The best way to do this is to separate out the cloves from the bulbs, but leave the papery coating on. You only need to plant the large ones; you can eat the small ones. Sort through them and remove any manky ones as they won't do well.

It is best to buy certified seed garlic to avoid the spread of disease. Store-bought garlic intended for eating is often treated to avoid the garlic sprouting in the store.

When spacing them out, if you think how big a garlic bulb is then you need to plant them about that far apart with a little room to spare so they need to be about 10–15cm apart.

You need to plant them deep as the bulb forms underground. The general rule of thumb is twice as deep as the clove is long. This is about 6cm. Make sure the pointy end is up and the flat end is down as this is where the roots will come out of.

If your garden isn't ready for a winter sowing or gets a bit soggy over the winter months, then you can start the garlic cloves off in containers and transplant them when the conditions are more suitable.

Make sure the soil stays moist in any dry periods over the winter and spring, but avoid watering in the few weeks before they are ready. Harvest when a third of the leaves start to die down after about six months.

Grow onions from seed.

Ready for harvest.

BEYOND THE GARDEN

After a season of success, it is very tempting to look around and think "hmm what else can I grow?" The spice aisle and whole food section in the store takes on a new light. Items that have lingered in the back of the pantry for far too long aren't immune to being considered as a possibility.

It is a fun thing to try. A good idea is to set aside a small part of the garden for these experimental crops. Although try to find out as much as you can about their growth habit first so you can support the plant as it grows. Be prepared for failure as seeds and other items intended for eating are often, but not always, treated to prevent them sprouting in the store.

Not all things are edible

As your gaze lifts from the store and the pantry and find yourself wondering about berries on trees and shrubs, potential mushrooms on the ground and other possible sources for the interesting and the unusual, I need to offer a very strong word of caution:

If you can't prove with 100% certainty that a plant is edible – don't even attempt to try it.

Blackberries are an autumnal treat.

Stay safe!

Don't eat any fungi unless you are certain what it is.

FORAGING

This is a great activity to involve the whole family on a day out, to gather free and edible items from the wild and there is plenty to be found. Some are as obvious as the sweet blackberries protected by their thorny branches. Others are subtler and it turns out the weed you have been fighting all season is actually quite nice to eat and can even have medicinal properties.

If you are going to do some gathering away from the garden, there are a few things to consider:

❉ Don't eat it if you don't recognise it.
❉ Make sure there are no spray residues and other pollutants on the plants.
❉ Don't take all that you see, leave some for the wildlife.
❉ Make sure you have permission where necessary.

There is a lot of useful information available out there for foraging in your area, so do your research.

TAKE NOTE

Where is your favourite place to forage?
Are there any unexpected edibles in your garden?
What usual things would you like to try and grow?

UNDERCOVER GARDENING

Sometimes the desire to garden can be strong in a gardener and the thought of an entire season stretching out with no hope of any really gardening other than racing in and out with frost cloth and trying to notice any growth on overwintering brassicas is just too much. For the keen gardener the season can be extended by growing under cover.

There are many options available from an elaborate and ornate glasshouse not dissimilar to a conservatory through to a few shelves wrapped in plastic to keep out the cold. There is something for everyone, depending on your budget, available space and what you want to achieve in the garden.

⁂ **Mini Greenhouses** can be readily purchased at an affordable price and are generally a set of shelves with a plastic cover. There is a word of caution with these – they are quite lightweight and can be whisked away in the slightest breeze. Secure it to a wall or fence or weigh it down with heavy objects and set it up in a sheltered spot for best success.

⁂ **Cloches** are small clear dome shapes that protect individual plants from the cold conditions. They can be a fancy moulded glass or a 3-litre juice bottle with the bottom cut off – each will work as well as the other.

⁂ **Garden bed cloches** can either be purchased or made and are an arch-shaped structure covered in plastic and installed directly over the garden. They can be as simple as a row covering or can enclose the entire garden bed.

⁂ **Cold frames** are a low permanent structure with clear roof where tender plants can be left to overwinter and can also be useful in the hardening off process or even as place to grow cold tolerant plants over the winter for an early harvest.

A plastic cover over a frame will help extend the growing season.

A Geodesic Bio Dome lets you grow in the coldest of weather.
Photo credit: Bren Haas at brenhaas.com

When using a light framed mini greenhouse, please **make sure you anchor it down well**. It is very upsetting to lose seedlings in a preventable greenhouse disaster.

✳ **Poly tunnels** are similar to the garden bed cloche only a lot bigger. This arch-shaped plastic lined structure is generally the size of a walk-in greenhouse or bigger and provides a spacious environment to garden in whatever the weather.

✳ **Aluminium-framed greenhouses** with polycarbonate panels are a more affordable form of glasshouse, however the panels make the structure much lighter and are more susceptible to storm damage.

✳ **Glasshouses** with glass panes are generally aluminium or wooden framed and are quite sturdy and permanent and it would take quite a storm to cause damage.

✳ **Geodesic Bio Dome** is a wonderful way to create an environment conducive to growing all year round – even in the depths of a snowy winter.

TAKE NOTE
WHAT IS GOING ON IN YOUR GARDEN THIS WEEK?

How do you keep your seedlings warm in the spring? How can you improve on this?

COOL WEATHER CRUNCH

As the weather closes in and there isn't much going on in the garden, the desire for something fresh can almost become like a craving. Here is a way to get a bit of fresh crunch, jam-packed full of nutrients and harvestable within a week or two.

Microgreens

Essentially small seedlings of many vegetable plants that are eaten before or just after their true leaves show. This works on the premise that no added nutrients are required as the nutrient provided in the seed is all that is needed. The time to harvest is just as this is beginning to run out for small seedling, where it would ordinarily seek out its own nutrients.

There is such a variety of microgreens.

1. In a shallow container or dish add your growing media and damp it down. You can use seed-raising mix, tissue paper or cotton wool as a base for growing microgreens. They won't be there long enough to worry about the medium they are growing in, just so long as it is able to stay moist and allow the roots to get some support as they grow.
2. Sow your seeds thickly and cover with a light layer of seed-raising mix, tissue or a cotton teased out to a very thin layer. Mist with water often to keep it all damp, but not soggy.
3. Once they reach the stage where the true leaves are beginning to emerge, take a pair of sharp scissors and snip them off at the base and add as a nutrient-packed garnish to your favourite meal.
4. They won't regrow after you harvest them so it is a good idea to start a new batch off regularly then you'll always have some on the go and you will always have some to harvest when you want it.

Seeds suitable are generally ones where you are able to eat the leaves of the mature vegetable or herb, so your choices for suitable microgreens is wide-ranging. You can try:

- Peas
- Brassicas
- Amaranth
- Fenugreek
- Fennel
- Rocket
- Beets
- Basil
- Coriander
- Dill
- Radish
- Mustards

Bean Sprouts

These are also the immature seedlings but they are grown in a different way and as the name suggests beans are the most common seed source although you can use others.

1. Start by adding enough seeds to generously cover the bottom of a large clean jar up to about a fifth of the jar.
2. Cover the jar with a cheese cloth, or similar mesh cloth, secured with a rubber band or even drill many holes in the jar lid.
3. Then fill the jar with water and leave to soak for eight to twelve hours. The larger the bean the longer they need. You will be able to tell if they have had enough as they will be all swollen.
4. Leaving the lid in place, drain away the water and rinse a couple of times and then drain again to make sure most of the water has gone.
5. Repeat this process of rinsing and draining at least twice a day.
6. Once the beans are about 3–5cm long, or however long you like to eat them – can take as little as three days or up to a week, rinse them one last time in a colander or sieve and remove any that haven't sprouted.
7. Store them in a sealed container with a paper towel to absorb moisture and also stop them from drying out and store them in the fridge. They should keep for several days.

You can try:
- Mung Beans
- Alfalfa Seeds
- Radish Seeds
- Whole Lentils
- Soy Beans
- Brassica Seeds
- Chickpeas
- Peas

Make sure everything you use is scrupulously clean to reduce the risk of food poisoning.

Sprouted mung beans.

TAKE NOTE
WHAT IS GOING ON IN YOUR GARDEN THIS WEEK?

What indoor crops have you tried? Did you enjoy them? How did you eat them?

EARLY WINTER

To some this may seem like the bleakest of seasons, however, if you look at it through the eyes of a gardener then we are closer to the start of the new growing season than we are to then end of the last one. All we need to do is wait patiently through the next few months, with the occasional pottering about in the garden while bundled up in warm clothes. This is a great time to enjoy the fruits of your labour as there is nothing quite like a rich homemade soup from vegetables you grew and stored away for days such as these.

Sow	*Plant*	*Maintain*	*Harvest*
• Outdoors – broadbean, cabbage, onion, and peas	• Plant seedlings of cabbage, cauliflower, broccoli, winter lettuce, spinach and silverbeet.	• Feed existing plants.	• Broccoli, Brussels sprouts, cabbage, carrot, cauliflower, leek, parsnip, radish, spinach, spring, swede and turnip
	• Plant asparagus crowns.	• Dig a large amount of compost and well-rotted manure through your vegetable garden to prepare for Spring.	
	• Plant garlic, shallots and onion sets.	• Cut back asparagus when stems turn yellow and apply compost.	NOTE: This is just a guide – things may happen faster or slower in your garden.
	• Plant rhubarb crowns.		
	• Plant strawberries.		

Winter can be a damp, bleak season.

CHOICES, CHOICES, CHOICES

Now you have a season of gardening behind you with a foundation in the basics of growing your own food, you may want to explore other options for growing food that may align with your personal philosophies, that may suit your situation, or you may just want to experiment and see what happens.

With a good basic knowledge any problems you encounter along the way will be solved much easier if you can determine if it is a common garden problem or something more complex involved with the style you have decided to use.

Aquaponics
A variation on hydroponics where plants are grown in aerated water however, the nutrients come from a fish tank where the fish provide the nutrients for the plants in the form of poop and in return the plants clean the water for the fish to live in. You still need to feed the fish and in some situations you can even eat the fish, but check the rules and regulations in your area for keeping fish like this as in some places the rules aren't suitable for farming fish in your backyard.

Companion Planting
This is almost like creating a harmonious community for plants not only to co-exist but making plants work together for a better outcome. It is like considering plants

Flowers and vegetables can make great companions.

have a social connection to one another – almost like people.

✳ Sometimes it is for physical benefits such as the three sisters method where sweetcorn stalks are used for beans to climb up, and the beans fix the nitrogen in the soil with the nodules on their roots and the large leaves on the pumpkin provide a mulch effect to reduce weeds and improve moisture retention.

* Plants can happily share space if the demands on the soil or need for sunlight are different from each other and they aren't competing.
* Other plants don't really like to hang out with others and release chemicals that inhibit the growth of other plants.
* Some are said to repel pests that can attack their neighbours.
* The strong smell of onion is supposed to confuse the sensitive nose of the carrot fly.
* There is even the possibility that the right combination of plants can improve the health and yield of the group. However, you may need to be guided by your own experiences as there is a lot of conflicting advice out there over which plants make the best neighbours.

There is no right or wrong way to grow vegetables – except not growing them at all.

TAKE NOTE
WHAT IS GOING ON IN YOUR GARDEN THIS WEEK?

How is the weather outside? How much time are you spending out in the garden?

Food Forests

This is a low-maintenance system that replicates the forest in nature with edible versions of the plants in each layer from the tallest fruit trees canopy to shrubs, ground covers and even root crops, all growing together in a three-dimensional ecosystem.

Hugelkultur

This is a great solution if you have poor soil with drainage issues. It is a raised bed built over a pile of rotting logs and organic material covered over with soil to plant into. It is almost like planting directly into your compost pile, with the added benefit

Hydroponics is a clean easy way to grow.

of a rich base once the logs rot down and due to the way the pile is constructed, the need for watering and fertilising the garden is reduced.

Hydroponics

This is a clean hands way of gardening, although it does initially require setting up specialised equipment. It is growing plants in nutrient enriched, aerated water that is

TAKE NOTE

WHAT IS GOING ON IN YOUR GARDEN THIS WEEK?

Is there a gardening style or two you would like to investigate further?

pumped past the roots of the plants. Once you are set up it is quite an easy technique as it eliminates many of the variables that come with growing in the soil.

Intensive Gardening

This is a technique used to get the most out of a small space, but starting with a very rich soil and then planting into every available space, not necessarily in rows. As soon as plants are removed then the space is reused with succession planting. Planting close together also keeps the weeds down, however reduced airflow can make closely planted crops more susceptible to pest and disease.

Lasagne Gardening

This is the ultimate no dig method of gardening. The structure of the garden is built up with alternating layers of brown and green materials not too dissimilar from how you should load your compost bin. It is preferable to put this garden together in the autumn to give the components a chance to break down, however, you can start out in the beginning of the growing season if you add a layer of soil or compost to the top.

Moon Planting

In ancient times this was one of the key methods to determine when and how to grow crops for many cultures. It relies on the gravitational effects of the moon on moisture on the soil. It was observed that plants sown at different stages of the moons cycle fared better than others sown at different times. The moon is divided into phases where the light is increasing

– waxing, or decreasing – waning. The basic premise is during the waxing phase the gravitational pull is stronger so it is a good time to plant things that produce their crops above ground and when it is waning the gravitational pull is much less so it is much suited to the crops that develop underground. There is much more to this technique including when is the best time to apply fertilizers, when to weed and when to just leave the garden alone. It would seem there is more to this than folklore and superstition as it has some scientific support as well.

There is a wealth of information available for the different styles of gardening from books to websites and even support groups. Don't be afraid to ask for advice.

No-Dig Method

Starting with a weed-free garden, a layer of good-quality compost or well-rotted animal manure is added to the top in autumn and left to be broken down by the elements so it is ready to plant in the spring. This is repeated each autumn to refresh the soil. It is important not to walk on the soil or disturb it in any way to avoid interrupting the balance of life within the soil. It is ensuring this ecosystem stays healthy that will ensure a healthy garden to be grown.

Organic Gardening

This system avoids the use of commercial and synthetic fertilizers and pest controls in order to produce food in a more natural way. It has a holistic approach from the way the soil is prepared, to how pests and disease are controlled and the use of beneficial insects and using seeds and seedlings known to be organic. Organic gardens can be more labour intensive than conventional gardening, but knowing the provenance of the food you are feeding your family can give you peace of mind.

Permaculture

By observing the way nature operates without the need of a gardener in order to have a productive outcome, this natural system has been developed to become a sustainable food production system by following similar principles of working with nature instead of trying to control it. The garden is designed to be a closed system where everything in the garden has a useful purpose and all waste gives back in some way. It can go beyond the garden and can incorporate animals and even become a way of life.

Square Foot Gardening

This a great solution if space is limited. It is based on a raised bed divided into equal grids. A certain number of plants can be grown within each grid, depending on what it is. Things are planted a little closer than normal, however the soil is prepared in a specific way to allow for this. It is a very orderly way to grow vegetables.

Straw Bale

Growing without soil in a straw bale can be an interesting alternative to conventional gardening, however you need to do your research before you start in order to have

Planting by the moon can influence growth.

Vertical gardening is a great solution for small spaces

a bountiful crop. The straw needs to be conditioned before beginning to grow in it and there are some questions as to the complete availability of nutrients for your plants. One of the benefits is it can be done on a hard surface such as a concrete driveway.

Vertical gardening

If space is limited, then utilising walls, fences and balcony rails for gardening spaces is a great solution. As urban living becomes more intensive then the desire to grow food in a lack of space has become a problem many inventive gardeners have developed solutions for and there are products available to suit most situations for those who want or need to grow vertically.

You may find other options available to try as you look for the method that suits you and your lifestyle. From sticking with the conventional to adapting a sustainable lifestyle, growing food for your family will always be a rewarding thing to do.

DEALING WITH FLOOD DAMAGE

The weather in winter is far from ideal and can cause havoc in the garden. A winter storm can test the strength of your structures and greenhouses and hopefully they survive the worst winter can throw at them. Broken structures are easily fixed or replaced, but when damage has been done to your soil, you need to proceed with caution so you don't want to cause lasting damage that will harm your ability to grow food in the future.

The biggest risk to the soil in winter is flooding. It can come from too much rain for too long or even worse, a river nearby bursting its banks. Having the soil saturated for an extended period is quite devastating to the plant and soil microbial life and not to mention the worms – they don't swim very well.

If you find yourself having to deal with the aftermath of serious flooding, you should:

Allow flooded soils to drain away before working.

* Avoid walking on the soil as much as possible and definitely don't try and dig or cultivate the soil. Wait for it to dry out.
* If there are precious plants you want to save, dig them up and put them in pots. Sitting about in sodden soil will quickly rot the roots.
* Harvest what crops you can before the plant drowns at the roots. Although depending on how the flooding occurred, there may be risk of contamination from pollutants and other not so pleasant things so wash thoroughly or maybe don't eat the veggies that don't get cooked.
* There is a chance the structure of your soil may be altered, or more devastating your top soil could have been washed away. A soil test for pH and NPK will give you a good idea of what has happened so you can make informed decisions as to how to rejuvenate the damaged soil. You may find the soil has become acidic as a result of the waterlogging so adding lime can help bring it back to a desirable level.
* Adding lots of organic material and compost will help to restore the microbial balance and incorporate structure to the compacted soil. Blood and bone will also help to improve the vitality of the soil.

If winter flooding is a common occurrence for you, once the garden gets back to normal, consider growing in raised beds or investigating ways to improve the drainage.

While it isn't ideal to walk on your fluffy well maintained soil at any stage, to avoid compaction, walking on the garden while it is wet or frozen can cause damage that can take quite some time to come right.

TAKE NOTE
WHAT IS GOING ON IN YOUR GARDEN THIS WEEK?

Have you ever had serious flooding in your garden? What can you do to reduce the risk of flooding?

....

....

....

....

GIVING THE GARDEN THE SUPPORT IT NEEDS

Gardens often need a little support, whether it's to keep a fragile plant from falling over, protecting the garden from strong winds or making better use of the space there are many options available. With the combination of many uses and many choices of structure you need to make sure what you choose to use actually does the job in your garden.

The kind of questions you should ask yourself are:
* What do I need this structure to do?
* How big will the plant I need to support get?
* What is the natural growth habit of the plant? – Does it have tendrils and likes to climb or am I training it to do something to make things easier for me?

Bamboo poles

These are a great natural resource and readily available to gardeners. They can be bound together to make wonderful structures to keep the garden in order. It is important to use string that will last the season and not rot away in the elements. Tie with strong knots. Cable ties are a strong, durable solution if your best knot tying is a dubious granny knot.
* Bean poles – Climbing beans like to twist themselves around a pole in a clockwise direction as they follow the sun and a bamboo pole makes an ideal support. Several poles lashed together can allow for the row to support itself from the dangers of falling over in high winds or when heavily laden with beans ready to pick.
* Even dwarf beans have a tendency to loll over under the weight of their harvest and so providing a short bamboo pole to lean against or be tied to can keep your beans from dragging on the ground.
* Tepees are an effective and aesthetically pleasing way to grow climbing beans and peas in the garden.
* Framing for netting – bamboo poles are handy to hold up netting in the garden as they can be easily woven through the net allowing it to be stretched out and secured into the soil.

Bamboo poles can last for a couple of seasons but you do need to watch them

Watch your eyes. If you are using short sticks and poles, it is a good idea to pop something over the top like an empty bottle or a ping pong ball, to reduce the risk of poking your eyes while working in the garden.

TAKE NOTE
WHAT IS GOING ON IN YOUR
GARDEN THIS WEEK?

How have your structures stood up to the
season? What would you do differently?
How will you store them over winter?

....

....

....

....

....

*Branches and sticks can
make an excellent support.*

for wear and tear. Check thoroughly for
cracking and weakness before using or you
will end up with your crop lying about
the base of a splintered pole that gave way
under the weight.

Netting and trellis

This is good for plants that have tendrils
and love to climb up, plants like peas and
cucumbers, so they can work their way up,
across and over the structure. There are a
few things to consider when providing a
netting structure.

* Firstly, you need to consider the size
  and weight of the mature plants. If your
  support structures holding the net in
  place aren't strong enough, then the risk
  is the netting will sag dreadfully under
  the weight or even be blown over in a
  bit of a wind.

* If the trellis isn't tall enough, then the
  plants can also be damaged by the
  wind at the tops as there is nothing to
  support it from being buffered about.

* The size of the holes in the netting can
  also be important, especially if you have
  it up against a fence or wall. If it is too
  small you may not be able to reach to
  the other side to harvest your crops.

Tomatoes

Left to their own devices the tomato
plant would sprawl across the ground,
making roots where the stems meet the
ground. However, this growth habit is not
convenient and having the leaves and fruit
so close to the soil, the risk of disease from
splashback is very high. So for a productive
outcome it is best to hold the tomato plant
hold upright against its will. Fortunately
for the gardener the options for restraining
wayward tomatoes are endless.

Ensure the supports holding up netting are strong.

One of the many ways to support tomatoes is to grow them up some wires.

* Tomatoes can be tied to a strong bamboo pole, however under the weight of a fully laden plant the risk of snapping at the base is quite high.
* They can have a cage popped over the top so they can have support as they grow, but it should be tall enough and the sides of the cage should have wide enough gaps to reach in to harvest the tomatoes. With this method you need to be aware of ensuring good airflow around the plant.

When tying in plants, try to use strips of soft cloth. String and wire can cut into the plant and damage it. Don't tie it too tight to allow for growth and gentle movement and cross over your tie between the plant and what you are tying it to so they don't rub together.

* Wire supports – if you have more than one tomato you may want to consider setting up a series of horizontal wires held in place with sturdy posts, and as the plant grows it is tied onto the wires.
* String may seem like a lightweight option however it is very effective in a greenhouse. If you secure the string to the base of the plant and to an overhanging structure, then as the plant grows the stem is wound around the string and the plant is held upright.

Decorative elements

Veggie gardens needn't be ugly or just utilitarian, support structures can be beautiful too. With the use of colour or items like obelisks, archways and wooden trellis the garden can be a lovely place to look out over.

The options for supporting your plants are only really limited by your creativity and is a fabulous opportunity for some recycling and upcycling.

MID-WINTER

This month is often fraught with restlessness for the keen gardener. It has been so long since hands were plunged into warm, crumbly soil. The temptation to just start a few seeds is very strong – to get a jump on the season. This should be avoided at all costs, it does more harm than good to the plant and the morale of the gardener as the plants will struggle to thrive. This is a time for dreaming not doing, while wrapped up warm in front of a blazing fire. Rest up because the busy times will soon be here.

Sow	*Plant*	*Maintain*	*Harvest*
• Outdoors – beetroot, broadbean, carrot, onion, parsnip, peas, silverbeet.	• Plant seedlings of onions, potatoes, rhubarb, silverbeet and cabbage. • Plant garlic, shallots and onion sets. • Plant asparagus crowns. • Plant strawberries.	• Digging in green manure cover crops. • Do not cultivate wet, boggy soils. • Prepare rhubarb and asparagus beds for planting.	• Broccoli, Brussels sprouts, cabbage, cauliflower, leek, spring onion, parsnip, spinach, swede and turnip NOTE: This is just a guide – things may happen faster or slower in your garden.

Mid-winter brings a chill that goes right through to the bone.

CROP ROTATION

Planning your first garden is easy, just decide where you want things to go, remembering tall plants at the back and short plants at the front, and you just plant your seedlings. The next time it gets a little more complicated because you have to take into consideration crop rotation.

To ensure you have a healthy garden for seasons to come, it isn't a good idea to plant things in the same place year after year. Different plants use the nutrients in the soil differently and by having the same plants in the same spot can result in deficiencies and an imbalance in the soil.

But worse than that you can end up with a build-up of pest and disease in the soil, that lie in wait for the new season, and any problems you have had would be back with vigour. By growing things in different places you can break the cycle of problems that you could face.

It is a good idea to give each spot a decent break from each type of crop, of up to four years as this can give pests and disease a decent length of time for populations to significantly decline to a level that wouldn't bother healthy crops. Even longer is even better.

So knowing things need to change is one thing, but you can't just pop them into a different spot willy nilly. You need to have an orderly plan so it is easy to keep track of where things have been and where

Easy tip – Just move the signs.

they need to go in the future. Just to make things more complicated some plants benefit from following some crops more than others.

Crop rotation is quite a thing to get your head around, especially if you want to incorporate companion planting in your garden. There are so many ways that this should be done with crops being divided into different groups and even suggestions that if you plant randomly in your small back yard garden with plants in no particular order you reduce the risk of soil borne diseases and nutrient deficiencies. However, there is still a risk of these diseases and it is better to make an informed decision about how you will grow your crops in the garden.

The best way to start is look at all the things you are growing and group them into families.

Even in a small garden just plant everything to the right of where it was last season.

✴ Tomatoes, peppers, potatoes and eggplant are all related. They are in the Solanaceae family. They are all susceptible to the dreaded blight so it is best to keep them together so if you encounter blight it is only restricted to one area of the garden and it is able to have a break from them for a few years to recover.

✴ Then you have your Brassicas. These are the broccoli, cabbage, cauliflowers, Brussels sprouts, kale, kohlrabi, but also radish, swede, turnip, rocket and mustard.

These are susceptible to the most awful disease – Clubroot. It is caused by a fungus in the soil. It makes the roots swell up and become disfigured and prevents them from doing their job of absorbing water and nutrients, which makes the plants stunted. If you get it there is no chemical control for this disease and although you can treat your soil to reduce the risk, you can never really get rid of this. The best thing to do is keep moving your brassicas to avoid the population of the fungus to build up to such an extent it becomes a problem. If you only rotate one family of plants, then this would be the one to move.

✴ Legumes are a great family because they do such good work in the soil with their nitrogen fixing nodules. These include peas, beans, peanuts, and the cover crop lupin. You want to move these about the

If you find you can't quite make it work allowing for tall plants to be at the back and short ones at the front, then have a couple of separate rotation cycles for the garden – the tall ones at the back and the short ones at the front and go from left to right in a crop rotation row rather than going around your garden in a circular fashion.

garden so their efforts can benefit all of the soil. It is a great idea to plant these where leafy greens or hungry plants will go next so the soil is enriched for them.

* The Allium family are thought to have beneficial properties that reduce the pests and disease in the soil. These are your garlic, onions, leeks, shallots and chives.

Then you have everything else, that individually can have their problems and bring benefit to the garden however collectively they don't compromise the long-term health of the garden. These can be divided into two groups:

* The crops you eat from above ground – spinach, sweetcorn, celery, pumpkin and zucchini, cucumbers and lettuce.
* The root vegetables that grow underground but aren't in any other high risk group, such as beets, carrots and parsnips.

An easy way to manage your crop rotation is to create signs for each group and at the beginning of each season just move the signs in the garden so you know what should go where!

Then there is even the suggestion that a part of the garden should lie empty for a year to allow it to recover. In an ideal world this would be lovely, but most people don't have the space for that.

Often the suggestion is to divide the garden into four groups and each year move them clockwise. Although as we have seen above we have come up with six groups – or seven if you want to leave a part of your garden empty. And of course it isn't as simple as just putting one after another in

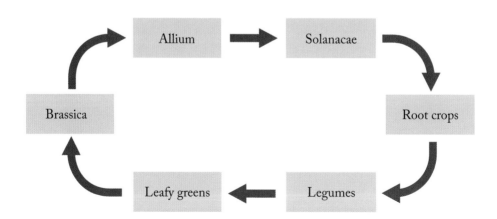

Avoid planting brassicas in the same place.

What changes do you need to make to
your plan to incorporate the crop rotation
principles?

a random fashion, you want each crop to
follow one another in a way that benefits
the one coming next.

Take potatoes for example – they are
good for breaking in new soil and don't like
it too rich. Carrots don't like a rich, firm,
lumpy soil and so having them follow the
potatoes makes sense because the ground
has already been dug over in search of
the potatoes. Legumes planted before the
leafy greens can give the soil a boost that
the leafy greens will love. Alliums before
the tomatoes may just reduce the risk of
diseases hiding in the soil so the tomatoes
get a good clean start.

So just thinking about the needs of the
plants gives it some kind of logical order.

Once you find a plan that works best
for you, putting it into practice couldn't be
easier. All you need to do when planning
your garden is to group them together and
then each year move the location clockwise
in the garden bed. At the very least to crops
won't be in the same spot in the garden for
at least six years.

At the end of the day there are many
variations to this complex task and so find a
system that suits you best. If push comes to
shove you can get away with leaving things
as they are for a year or two at most, but
anything beyond that is putting the success
of your garden at risk.

ASPARAGUS

The crown of a year old asparagus.

Growing asparagus takes some commitment as you can't eat any in the first season, and in the second you can have a few, but by the third season you can eat them to your heart's content from the first spear that pops up in the early spring, until early summer, by which time you'll probably be sick of the sight of them. It is definitely worth the effort and all the waiting as not only is it a long lived plant and will come back every year for a good twenty years, but fresh asparagus is absolutely amazing. It is so sweet and delicious and tastes nothing like the ones you can buy.

So you remember where your young asparagus is at, pop a marker beside each 1 year crown that says "Don't eat me" and beside your 2 year crowns "Have a few".

All good garden centres should sell asparagus crowns in the winter months and they look a little bit like an octopus – if you have a little imagination.

✳ They need to be planted in a sunny spot with well-drained soil.

✳ Make sure it is definitely where you want them to be as once they are established it is difficult to move them and they will be there for a very long time.
✳ Dig a trench about as wide and as deep as your spade and make a ridge of good rich soil along the base of the trench.
✳ Spread the asparagus crown out over ridge separating all the 'tentacles.'
✳ Cover with about 5cm of soil and then as the asparagus grows in the spring, slowly fill in the rest of the trench until it is level with the surface of the garden.

All that is left to do is wait patiently, but I assure you, it is worth it.

The taste of fresh asparagus is like nothing else.

TAKE NOTE
WHAT IS GOING ON IN YOUR GARDEN THIS WEEK?

What temperature does it reach in the day? How cold does it get at night? What are you harvesting? What do you enjoy most about your garden?

STRAWBERRIES

As much as it would seem like winter is entirely composed of rain, snow, wind and freezing temperatures, there are still some amazing days where the sky is blue. By avoiding the wind chill factor, the sun can reach through and feel warm upon your face. These are perfect gardening days and it is on days like these we can make all the necessary preparations for one of the greatest things the early summer has to offer – strawberries!

Having strawberries in the garden is like growing candy. Strawberry plants are available in most good garden centres throughout the winter months and all you need to do is plant them into a rich soil, with loads of good compost and well-rotted vegetarian animal poop. You need to make sure the ground you have chosen doesn't get too wet and boggy as strawberries hate getting wet feet. Luckily they don't mind growing in containers and there are loads of different types of containers designed specifically with strawberries in mind.

The things you need to watch out for with strawberries is:

At the end of the season strawberry plants will put out runners. These can be encouraged to root and then you will end up with many new plants.

* If you grow them in the ground they can rot if they come in contact with the soil, so it is best to lay down a mulch of straw, pea straw or untreated sawdust.
* You will also need to compete with others to get your ripe strawberries, Birds are notorious strawberry thieves and the best way to protect your crop is to secure a net firmly around your plants. Before you know it, the cold winter day spent planting your strawberries will be a distant memory as you bite into that first red juicy berry and you'll know it was time well spent.

Growing strawberries is like growing candy.

Strawberries only really fruit well for three years, so divide your crop into thirds and each year replace a third and you will always have plants producing at their best.

PATIENCE

There are times in the garden there is so much to do and you feel like there aren't enough hours in the day and days in the week. Each time you cross something off the 'To Do' list another five things are added to the bottom. There is a satisfaction in working so hard, seeing the garden come to life under your tending and care.

Then there are other times when there doesn't seem to be much to do at all. Waiting for the seedlings to grow, waiting for the frosts to stop and the soil to warm up, waiting for the harvest to ripen and even waiting for one crop to finish so you can plant another. And then there is now – in the middle of the middle month of winter where not a lot can be done and the start of the season seems impossibly far away.

Not everything you read on the internet is true so verify any advice found or received by checking with reliable sources – advice from a commercial brand, academic institute or respected horticultural organisation.

Make sure information you find is specific to your area where applicable, for example pests and disease diagnoses.

The waiting times are filled with anticipation and the temptation to just hurry things along, however this is counterproductive. If you must fill your time with all things gardening, then take the time to learn.

* Learn about the growing conditions in your area.
* Join garden groups and local online communities.
* Subscribe to magazines and newsletters that will help guide you through the seasons with trusted timely advice, wisdom and stories.
* Look to the internet for the latest research and discoveries regarding growing vegetables. This is an evolving world and staying informed can help improve your experience in the garden.
* Find videos and blogs online to show how others grow their food. This is useful for understanding just how an unfamiliar plant will grow, will help to explore the ups and downs of growing in different styles and also help you learn from the mistakes of others.
* Find out as much as you can about each plant you have decided to grow so you can provide the right conditions and know what to expect during the growing season.

There is so much information to be found.

* Review the notes you took all season and come up with a plan to integrate them into your new growing season.
* Go back through this book to refresh yourself for the season to come.

Try not to be swayed by the opinions of others if it doesn't suit your chosen gardening philosophy. There are many variations out there to go from seed to harvest and so long as you end up with something to eat then you're doing the right thing.

TAKE NOTE
WHAT IS GOING ON IN YOUR GARDEN THIS WEEK?

Where are your favourite places to go to find further information?

APPENDICES

But wait there's more.

Starting a garden is a journey that is without end. There is always next season and the hope that things will bigger, better and there will be more to learn and more to try. Once you start you will find it hard to stop. Once a gardener always a gardener.

Once you have reached the end of this book having gardened alongside it for the last year, you should now feel confident to go it alone and build on all you have learnt to become a confident and successful gardener. As a parting gift you will find great resources on the following pages to enhance your gardening expertise.

All the best with your future gardening endeavours.

Happy Gardening!

Growing Beans

How much space:

Between plants: Between rows:

How Tall:

Dwarf:

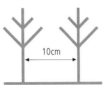
10cm

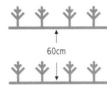
60cm

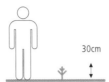
30cm

Climbing:

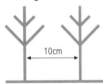
10cm

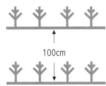
100cm

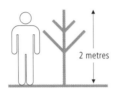
2 metres

How long before the harvest: 8 weeks

Dwarf: Grows in a small bush shape and doesn't need support.

Mound up the soil around the base as it grows to give extra support. No trellis needed as they can hold their own.

Climbing: Grow like a vine and needs support for it to grow up.

These wind themselves around a pole in an anticlockwise direction and won't need tying in.

Provide individual bamboo poles or a framework structure for them to grow up.

These seeds do best sown directly in the garden but can be transplanted if your garden isn't quite ready but by now it should be.

If the soil gets too wet before the seed emerges, the seed could rot.

You will have the best results when the temperature is over 20°C so there is no advantage to be gained by sowing them too early.

Dwarf beans: If the weather is cloudy for days on end then long tendrils may grow making you think it has reverted to a climbing variety. Just cut these off.

When to harvest:

Pick them when they are young and tender before the pods become lumpy as the seeds inside form.

The more you pick the more you get and so they will continue to flower and grow beans so long as you keep picking them.

Common problems:

- Nibblers – Slugs and snails.
- Suckers – Aphids, green vegetable bug.
- The best option is generally to spray as a prevention and a remedy.

Bean seeds

Beans

Bean seed leaves

Bean true leaves

Bean flower

Beans in different colours

Growing Broccoli, Cabbage and Other Brassicas

How much space:

Between plants: Between rows:

How Tall:

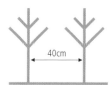
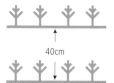
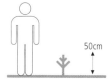

40cm   40cm   50cm

How long before the harvest: 10 weeks

Brassicas like firm soil so tread on the soil – not until it is compacted and impossible to poke your finger into, but so it is firm. This is known as 'the gardeners shuffle!'

Dig a hole slightly bigger than the root ball and fill it with water and let it drain away. Repeat several times. This is called 'puddling' and also gives your plants a good start.

Don't let brassicas dry out as there is a high chance they will bolt straight to seed.

Next season put them in a different spot in the garden to avoid diseases in the soil like Club Root.

Common problems:

- Nibblers – Slugs and snails, white cabbage butterfly.
- Suckers – Aphids, green vegetable bug, whitefly.

Broccoli seeds

Broccoli

Broccoli seed leaves

Broccoli true leaves

Broccoli seedling

Puddling

Growing Carrots

How much space:

Between plants: Between rows:

How Tall:

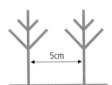
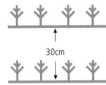
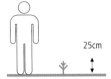

5cm   30cm   25cm

How long before the harvest: 16 weeks

These seeds need to sown directly in the garden. They won't do well as transplants.

Don't add any more organic material or compost to the row where you will plant your carrots. Carrots **hate** fresh organic matter! This can cause the weird shaped carrots.

Remove all lumps and stones, sticks and anything that can get in the way of a growing carrot. If the carrot hits an obstacle in the soil, then it will fork.

Don't weed around your carrots until the seedlings start producing their true leaves and looks like carrot tops, as the seed leaves look a lot like grass!

Feed with a liquid vegetable feed every couple of weeks for extra healthy plants.

Thinning:

Once they get going pull out carrots in the row to give a gap of about 2cm between carrots.

About a month later thin out again so the gap is about 5cm between the carrots. These will be your final carrots.

Don't throw away the thinings as you can eat them as baby carrots.

Every three to four weeks sow another row, so that by the time your first row has been eaten then your next one will be ready.

When to harvest:

Pull the soil back around the neck of the carrot to see how wide it is to tell if it is ready.

Pushing down on the carrot before pulling can help ease it out of the soil.

You don't need to dig them all up at once, just pull them out as you need them.

Common problems:

• Nibblers – Slugs and snails, carrot fly.

• Disease – Rust.

Carrot seeds

Carrot

Carrot seed leaves

Carrot true leaves

Carrot ready to harvest

Growing Cucumber

How much space:

Between plants: Between rows:

How Tall:

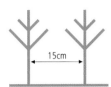
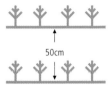
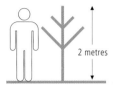

15cm   50cm   2 metres

How long before the harvest: 10 weeks

Growing them in trays indoors is how you can get a head start on the season.

Cucumber plants and the seeds don't like it when it is too cold and will sulk and even die so avoid planting them out too early. The soil should be 20°C or warmer to be successful.

Cucumbers have a sprawling growth habit and you could just let them ramble through your garden, but they also have tendrils and this indicates that they make excellent climbers.

When the plant is young it needs a little help hanging on to the trellis and can be threaded through the netting or loosely tied to the support

You can direct the growth of the plant so that it winds across the trellis or netting in a zig zag fashion or goes around the tee pee instead of straight up it so it doesn't get too high.

It is best to water this plant at the soil and not on the leaves or you will encourage mildew to form.

Common problems:

- Nibblers – Slugs and snails.
- Suckers – Aphids, green vegetable bugs.
- Disease – Powdery mildew.

Cucumber seeds

Cucumbers

Cucumber seed leaves

Cucumber true leaves

Young cucumber flower

Growing Lettuce

How much space:

Between plants: Between rows:

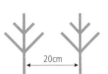 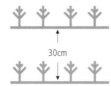

20cm   30cm

How Tall:

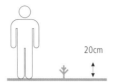

20cm

Lettuce seeds

How long before the harvest: 7 weeks

Lettuce don't actually like it all that hot and can go bitter and bolt to seed in the hottest days of summer. To lessen the effect, you can provide it with some shading.

Start off new seeds every two weeks throughout the summer to avoid bitterness and bolting and replace the plants you have eaten.

When to harvest:

With the cut and come again type you can pick leaves from around the outside of the plant. The middle leaves will continue to grow and you can keep picking them until you use it all up or the flavour becomes bitter.

The varieties that form a head are ready to pick once it feels firm when gently squeezed.

Common problems:

• Nibblers – Slugs and snails.
• Suckers – Aphids.
• Problems – Rotting and bolting.

Salad

Lettuce seed leaves

Lettuce true leaves

Heart lettuce

leaf lettuce

Growing Peas

How much space:

Between plants: Between rows:

How Tall:

Dwarf:

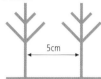
5cm

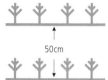
50cm

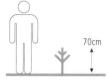
70cm

Climbing:

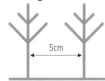
5cm

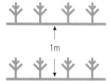
1m

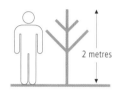
2 metres

How long before the harvest: 9 weeks

Dwarf: Grows in a small bush shape. A little support can help.

Climbing: Grows very tall and needs support for it to grow up.

Peas have tendrils to cling to support structures.

Tips:

Resist all temptation to water the row before the seedlings pop up as the seeds will rot if it is too wet.

Use trellis or poke a load of sticks and twigs into your row so the peas have something to hang onto as they grow or you may have to harvest your peas from off the ground.

Having peas in close contact with the soil makes them susceptible to soil borne diseases.

Cut the old vines off at the base and leave the roots in the soil as they have nitrogen rich root nodules that will enrich your soil as they break down.

When to harvest:

The more you pick the more, the more you get.

You should be able to tell when to pick them as the pods will become fat and plump. If they go a bit wrinkly, then they have gone too far.

Make sure you pick every single one or the plant will think it has done its job of setting seed and stop making anymore!

The whole pod of immature peas and tender pea shoots can be eaten.

Common problems:

- Nibblers – Slugs and snails, leaf miner, caterpillars.
- Suckers – Aphids.
- Disease – Mildew.

Pea seed

Peas

Pea seed leaves

Pea true leaves

Pea flower

Pea pods

Growing Peppers

How much space:

Between plants: Between rows:

How Tall:

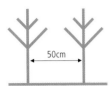 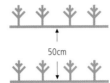 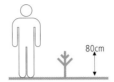

50cm

50cm

80cm

Pepper seeds

How long before the harvest: 12 weeks

These seeds do best sown indoors in seed trays as early in spring as possible as they need a long growing season.

The seeds are fickle and like it warm and won't germinate below 22°C and a good place to start them off is the hot water cupboard or on top of the fridge.

Put a short bamboo pole or stake beside each one when planting them out as they tend to get a bit of a lean on them, especially when they are laden with fruit.

Feed regularly once they have begun flowering.

Warning: wash your hands after handling the chilli fruit and don't touch yourself anywhere!

These plants are actually perennial and in the right climate last for several years. It is the frost that kills them. You can over-winter them in a greenhouse or sunny spot inside and then plant them out in the spring to get a great head start next season.

Red pepper

Pepper seed leaves

Pepper true leaves

Pepper flower

When to harvest:

The more you pick the more will come.

You can pick them at any stage, they don't need to be big like the store-bought ones, they can be picked small too.

Both chillies and peppers can be picked if they are green or red. The only difference is the flavours. The red ones are sweeter and in the case of the chilli will be hotter.

Common problems:

• Nibblers – Slugs and snails, caterpillars.

• Suckers – Aphids, green vegetable bug.

• Problems – Frost.

Green Peppers

Growing Sweetcorn

How much space:

Between plants: Between rows: **How Tall:**

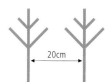
20cm

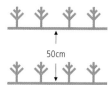
50cm

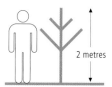
2 metres

How long before the harvest: 12 weeks

Sweetcorn seeds do better planted in a block, rather than in a row because it ensures the pollination has the best chance of resulting in full corn cobs.

The pollen is on the male tassels at the top and it falls on to the silky tassels about halfway down the stalk. Each silk is connected to individual kernels within the cob.

Sweetcorn is a tall crop and needs a strong deep anchor so it stands up to the winds that will buffer it. It's best to water deeply once or twice a week to encourage its shallow roots to go down deeper.

Another way to help the sweetcorn withstand the wind is to pull the soil up around the base of the plant.

Due to its rapid growth sweetcorn is a hungry and thirsty plant.

When to harvest:

Sweetcorn is ready when the silks go all brown and crispy and the cob will be poking out from the stalk. You can also peel back the husk and poke one of the kernels – if there is juice and it is creamy then the sweetcorn is perfect.

Common problems:

- Nibblers – Slugs and snails, Corn Ear Worms.
- Suckers – Aphids.
- Disease – Rust.

Sweetcorn ready to harvest

Sweetcorn seed

Sweetcorn cobs

Sweetcorn seed leaves

Sweetcorn true leaves

Sweetcorn tassles

Sweetcorn silks

Growing Tomatoes

How much space:

Between plants:

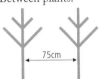

75cm

Between rows:

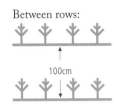

100cm

How Tall:

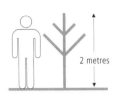

2 metres

How long before the harvest: 12 weeks

Tomato seeds

Tomatoes can grow very tall and ripening fruit can be quite heavy so they need support.

A strong stake, a cage or trellis are great options.

When tying to the support use a soft fabric and twist it between the post and the plant to avoid rubbing.

Tomatoes

Indeterminate: These plants tend to keep growing and producing until the first frost.

Determinant: These are generally bush varieties that will reach a certain size and then produce all their fruit at once.

Laterals:

Tomatoes need good airflow to remain healthy. So it is a good idea to remove the laterals – the branches that grow out from the stem at a 45° angle above a leaf. Use clean pruners or pinch out.

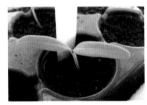

Tomato seed leaf

Flowers:

Tomato flowers are self-fertile which means the male and female parts are found within the flower and a gentle breeze is enough to pass the pollen from the male part to the female part and the tomato grows from there.

Tomato true leaf

Common pests:

- Nibblers – Slugs and snails, caterpillars and birds.
- Suckers – Whitefly, aphids, green vegetable bug and Psyllid.
- The best option is generally to spray as a prevention and a remedy.

Common diseases:

- Blight – brown patches on leaves, stems and fruit. Humid weather is often the cause. You may need to remove plants to avoid spreading.
- Botrytis – a grey mould on plant – poor airflow. Improve ventilation to reduce risk.

Common problems:

- Splitting fruit – inconsistent watering.
- Blossom end rot – lack of calcium & inconsistent watering.
- Curly leaves – wide difference in day / night temperatures.

Tomato lateral

Tomato flower

Growing Zucchini

How much space:

Between plants: Between rows:

How Tall:

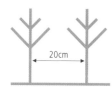
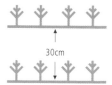
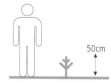

20cm   30cm   50cm

Zucchini seeds

How long before the harvest: 5 weeks

Planting outside:

Make a mound about 15–30cm high and about 30–60cm wide with a shallow well in the centre. Water deeply and leave for 10 minutes. Sow a couple of seeds no deeper than 3cm and cover.

Once the seedlings come through, remove the weakest one.

Zucchini and pumpkin seeds have a reduced risk of rotting if you plant them on their narrow side.

It is best to water this plant at the soil and not on the leaves or you will encourage mildew to form.

These plants tend to sprawl. The growth habit is generally one central stalk (although you can get more) that grows along the ground putting out flowers and zucchini all the way along as the season progresses. It normally ends up being a metre or so long.

The zucchini has male flowers and female flowers and the pollen from the male flower needs to get to a female flower so they can make baby zucchinis. This is usually done by bees.

Male flowers have straight stems. Female flowers have a swelling under the flower and if this is pollinated it will turn into the zucchini.

Zucchini fruit

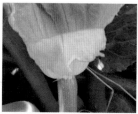

Zucchini female flower

Zucchini male flower

Zucchini seed leaves

When to harvest:

You can eat the flowers which can slow the harvest.

It is best to pick zucchini when they are small as they will grow enormous if you leave them.

They will turn into marrows if left, which are still edible and are really nice stuffed with a meatloaf mix and baked in the oven.

Common problems:

- Nibblers – Slugs and snails.
- Suckers – Aphids.
- Disease – Powdery mildew, blossom end rot.

Young zucchini plant

Zucchini true leaves

OTHER VEGETABLE GROWING ADVICE

Beetroot

These are a versatile vegetable and can grow almost all year round, from Late Winter to Early Autumn. The seed looks big but it actually a cluster of three to four seeds. Soaking it for a few hours before sowing can help with germination. They can be started either in seed trays indoors or directly in the ground. They don't seem to mind, but they don't like soggy soil. Plant them out 10cm apart in rows 25cm apart. They form above the soil so you can watch them grow and they should be ready in about ten weeks and about the size of a golf ball or bigger. Although don't let them get too big or they can become a bit woody and not nice to eat.

Beetroot.

Eggplant (Aubergines)

This is related to tomatoes and potatoes and come in many shapes and colours beyond the purple pendulous variety often seen in stores. Seeds should be started indoors in early spring indoors as they need a long, hot growing season. Plant them out with 75cm space around them and pop in a stake as they may need support. Eggplants grow about 90cm tall. They are perfectly suited to growing in a greenhouse if your summer is less than ideal. The fruit begin to be ready for harvest around mid-late summer. They are ready when they have a deep, rich colour and smooth skin. If the skin is wrinkly they have gone too far. Take cared when picking them as there are spikes on the calyx around the top. It is best to use pruners. You should get up to eight eggplants per plant.

Leek

The main aim of growing leeks is to get a lovely long white stem. It is best to start them off in a seed tray or out in the garden in a nursery bed and grow them on until they are about 20 cm tall or almost the width of a pencil. Lightly firm the soil and then using a dibber or the end of your rake, poke holes in the soil 15cm deep and 20cm apart. Pop the leek seedling into the hole and fill it full of water. As the water drains away it will wash soil down onto the roots. As the leek grows it will fill the hole and light will be excluded and you will get the desirable white stem. It takes up to fourteen weeks before it is ready to harvest, although you can dig them up sooner if you want tender young stems. They can be stored in the ground until needed.

Parsnip

As a long root crop these should be sown directly into the soil. It should be light and fluffy with a good compost or organic matter dug in. They can be a bit temperamental with germination so make sure you have the freshest seeds possible. Pouring boiling water over the seeds is said to help with germination. Patience is required as they can take up to four weeks to germinate. Once they do pop up, thin them to about 7cm apart. The leaves can be quite lush so allow 40cm between the rows. It takes up to twenty weeks to be ready however, it is best to leave them in ground until frost. The parsnip creates a kind of antifreeze by converting its stored starch to sugar, which makes it sweet and delicious to eat. They can be stored in ground all winter, but should be eaten before spring or they'll start to sprout again and become woody and won't taste nice.

Planting leeks.

Pumpkin (winter squash)

These need a lot of space as they tend to sprawl. Allow a metre space around where you want to grow them but you may find they grow beyond this. Smaller pumpkins can grow upwards. They can tolerate locations with shade for up to half a day down and you can't leave a mark when you try to pierce the skin with your thumbnail. Make sure you leave a long stalk. Wash them with a 10% bleach solution and then allow to cure in a dry sunny spot for two weeks, then store in a cool, dry place.

Pumpkin.

and are quite hungry plants so make sure the soil is very rich soil. You can plant them where you want them to grow or indoors – seeds in situ or indoors. The seedlings grow quite quickly so don't start indoors any earlier than a month before the last frost. Wait until it is warm enough to plant out or it will sulk. When sowing directly make sure all risk of frost has passed and the soil is warm or your plants will sulk and suffer. Pumpkins need up to six months to see a harvest and need to be well watered. Make sure you avoid splashing on leaves. You can slip some cardboard or something underneath the pumpkin to stop the fruit rotting. Harvest when the leaves have died

Spinach

This a great cool season crop which doesn't really like the heat of summer and will bolt. However, there are different varieties that suit different conditions so they can almost be grown year round. Make sure they are in rich soil and are well fed and watered to maintain their spinach flavour or they can become bitter. Space them about 30cm apart. Harvest the outside leaves in a cut and come again fashion and sow new seeds every 3–4 weeks to ensure a continual supply. It takes about ten weeks to be ready for picking – but you can take them earlier than that if you are after the tender baby leaves.

Silverbeet (Swiss Chard)

This plant is related to beetroot and comes in a wonderful array of bright colours. They are a great cut and come again crop that can grow for most of the year. The seed is actually a cluster of 3–4 seeds and can be sown directly in the garden or indoors in seed trays. Soaking the seeds for a few hours before sowing can help with germination. They can get quite big so allow 40cm all around. Feed with nitrogen rich fertilizer during the growing season to keep the plant healthy. Pick outside leaves in a downward twisting action, but don't strip the plant – leave half a dozen leaves in the centre.

Turnips and Swedes

These can be considered an old-fashioned vegetable, but are a fabulous crop for a cool season harvest. Turnips take up to twelve weeks to grow and swedes need a longer time and will be ready in about four months. Sow them directly in the garden about 10cm apart and in rows of 30cm apart. They are great candidates for succession sowing to extend the harvest. They mostly grow above the soil as they are formed from a swollen stem. Golf ball-sized is ideal, but don't let them get much bigger than a tennis ball. If you leave them in too long they can become quite fibrous and not a pleasure to eat. These are related to the cabbage family so consider this in your crop rotation and don't allow them to dry out or they will bolt to seed.

Radish

This is a fast crop and is best sown directly into the soil. It is related to the cabbage family so consider this in your crop rotation. They should be planted 5cm apart in rows away. It is often suggested to sow radish to help space out carrots – but this can result in an excessive number of radish. They best way to have a continuous supply of spicy crunchy goodness is to sow them little and often throughout the growing season. Keep them evenly moist to avoid splitting. Harvest after about 6–8 weeks and no bigger than a ping pong ball. They can go woody quite quickly if they get too big or too old.

Radish.

SPEAKING GARDENESE

Aside from being able to grow a bountiful harvest, what about sounding like an expert? Your friends and neighbours will see your lovely garden and will ask your advice and gardeners are friendly people and willingly share seedlings, excess crops and knowledge.

Here is a list of gardening terminology for you that will give you some extra knowledge and will give you the ability to drop 'photosynthesis' into a conversation with confidence.

This is certainly not all the gardening terms by any stretch of the imagination, but they are interesting to know or will be helpful for your veggie growing journey.

Acid: Measured using the pH scale. Acid is between 0 and 7. Soil that is too acid makes the nutrients too soluble and they get washed away.

Alkaline: Measured using the pH scale. Alkaline is between 7 and 14. Soil that is too alkaline holds on to the nutrients too tightly for the plants to access.

Allelopathic: This is a great word that rolls off the tongue. It is where the plant produces a chemical that makes it difficult for other plants to survive in the same area. A walnut tree is a great example. Nothing much grows under a walnut tree.

Annual: Most vegetables are annuals. This means they only last one season and set seed and finish their life cycle.

Biennial: These are plants that last two years. The first year they establish themselves and the second year they flower and set seed. Parsley is a biennial.

Catch Crop: A quick-maturing crop that can be grown between slower crops or between the harvest of one plant and the sowing of the next.

Chlorophyll: Pigment that makes plants green and important for photosynthesis.

Chlorotic: This is when the plant looks sick and yellow. There are many reasons that could cause this.

Cold-hardy: Plants that can survive cold and subfreezing temperatures and bounce back to grow again next season.

Compost: A nutrient-rich soil conditioner made from blend of one part nitrogen rich green garden and kitchen waste and two parts carbon rich brown garden waste, paper and cardboard that has rotted down and added to the soil to improve the quality.

Crown: The part of long-term plant that is found at soil level where the roots and stems grow from. This is generally the part you plant when growing asparagus or rhubarb.

Cultivar: The result of a natural plant from the wild that is grown in captivity – i.e. cultivated.

Cutting: A horticultural propagation technique used to grow copies of plants from a section of stem, root or leaf.

Dead-heading: Cutting off old flowers. This can cause new growth and new flowers and make the plant look pretty.

Determinate: Mostly applies to tomatoes, they are a more compact plant and the fruit pretty much all comes at the same time.

Dibber: A blunt pointy stick used to make holes in the soil for transplanting seedlings.

Division Propagation: This is when you dig up a plant and split it up for replanting to increase the number of plants you have. Not all plants are suitable for this, but rhubarb is a good example.

Drawn: The technical term for pale leggy seedlings that are reaching for the light.

Drill: The line you draw in the soil to plant fine seeds into.

Earthing up: Pulling the soil up around plants to exclude light. Especially important with potatoes so they don't go green. Green potatoes are toxic.

Edible: Plants that are safe to eat. If you aren't sure, do some research, especially when doing a bit of foraging.

Ericaceous: Used to describe acid-loving plants and acid soil.

F1: These seeds come from crossing two different parents, but the seed will have a reliable crop with specific qualities. However, there is no point saving seeds from these as the offspring will be a wild child and will have a dubious outcome.

Fasciation: When stems grow fused together. This is not normal.

Fertiliser: Blend of chemicals needed by the plant for healthy growth. This can be derived from natural or artificial sources.

Forcing: The technique of making plants fruit or flower earlier than they would naturally do it.

Genus: Closely related plants. Used in part of the scientific name for plants i.e. the potato is formally known as *Solanum tuberosum, Solanum* being the genus.

Germinate: This is what happens when the seeds wake up and begin to grow. It is usually started when the seed is exposed to moisture and warmth.

Ground Cover: Plants that grow to cover the ground.

Guttation: This is really cool when you see it. It is when sap from the xylem leaks out of the edges of leaves to form pretty droplets.

Half hardy: Plants that don't like frost but could survive a mild winter.

Harden-off: This is when you gradually get your indoor seedlings used to living on the outside.

Hardy: Plants that can handle a frost.

Heeling In: This is handy to know. If you buy plants because you saw them and just had to have them, but don't have anywhere for them to go. Ideally you should prepare the ground then buy the plant. But by popping them into a trench and lightly cover them over, so they can survive until you are ready to plant them where you want them to be.

Heirloom: These are seeds that have been handed down from generation to generation and are considered to be stable and reliable enough to repeat a similar harvest each year.

Herbaceous: A plant that dies back during the winter. It often has soft tissue not woody stems. Rhubarb is an example of this.

Humus: The material left after compost has finished decomposing completely.

Hybrid: A plant that has parents from a different species, but usually the same genus.

Indeterminate: This most commonly applies to tomatoes where the plant continues to grow and fruit all season until taken out by frost or disease.

Infestation: When a plant becomes overrun with pest or disease.

Inorganic: Materials not derived from living things.

Lateral: In a tomato plant this is the leaf that grows out of the stem where the leaf connects to the stem.

Leaching: When rain water washes away all the nutrients from the soil.

Mycorrhizum: The fine threadlike part of soil fungi. Most of them are beneficial and form great relationships with the plants. Others can spread disease.

Nodule: Occurs on the roots of some plants and work together with special bacterial to turn nitrogen in the soil to a form the plants can use.

Organic: Materials derived from living things.

Perennial: Plants that can live for more than two years. A pepper plant is actually a perennial in its original environment, but we treat it as an annual because it can't cope with the frost. If you take one inside, then you can grow it through the winter you will be able to harvest peppers earlier in the season.

Petrichor: The lovely smell of earth after rain.

Phloem: The cells within the plant that together form a transportation system taking food from the leaves.

Photosynthesis: How the plant converts carbon dioxide and water to sugar and oxygen using the sunlight.

Pollinate: In order to get most of our food, the flowers plants produce need to be pollinated. This requires the pollen from the male flower bits to be transferred to the female flower bits so the fruit is able to grow. This is normally transferred by bees, insects and the wind.

Potting mix: A commercially blended mix of soils, nutrients and materials that provide for a healthy home for plants grown in containers. It is disease-free and is able to retain moisture between watering for the plants to use.

Propagation: Plant reproduction by seed, cuttings or division.

PVR or PBR: Plant Variety Rights or Plant Breeders Rights. This means legally the grower of a new variety of plant owns the right to sell or propagate the plant and so you aren't allowed to save the seeds to sell or sell seedlings or cuttings. You should see PVR or PBR on the label in garden centres.

Scarification: Some seeds need to be treated in different ways before it will germinate. Techniques include but aren't limited to soaking, nicking with a craft knife, freezing or surviving a bush fire.

Self – Pollination: When the pollen fertilizes its own flower or the other flowers on the same plant and so doesn't need more than one plant to set fruit.

Species: Individual groups within a family. Used in part of the scientific name for plants i.e. the potato is formally known as *Solanum tuberosum, tuberosum* being the species.

Sucker: Vigorous branches the plant puts out to increase its size. Normally unwanted by gardeners as it will occur below a graft in a tree, or out of the stem of a tomato plant which can reduce airflow around the plant.

Tendril: A thin specialised stem that clings to nearby objects for support.

Tilth: A crumbly soil texture suitable for planting in. A fine tilth is perfect for sowing seed.

Transplant: To move a plant growing in a pot to a bigger pot or into the ground.

Trench: A long hole usually dug to the depth and width of a spade in the garden.

Tubers: These are stems that have adapted to be underground storage organs for the plant and we come along and eat them as potatoes or sweet potato. Note: not all tubers are edible.

Weed: A plant growing in the wrong place.

Xylem: The cells within the plant that together form a transportation system taking nutrients from the roots.

Beans in the summer sun.

WHAT IS WRONG WITH MY PLANT?

As lovely as it would be to have a perfect garden with healthy plants, because we are dealing with the variable that is nature, things will go wrong. Sometimes the solution can be as simple as giving the plant something to eat, and other times it may be more dramatic and would require ripping out the plant and burning it.

It can be quite daunting to be staring at a sick plant and have no idea what to do about it. Narrowing down the cause can often be quite simple and a process of elimination. The following is a guide to figuring out what is wrong.

However, there are things you should be aware of.

❋ Sometimes what you see isn't actually the problem but an attack from an opportunistic pest or disease taking advantage of a weak plant.

❋ Some problems are actually quite serious for the plant and for the long-term health of your garden, so if you believe you have a nasty problem, seek out professional advice for a second opinion and follow the recommended treatment immediately.

❋ If you have a nutrient deficiency, be very careful amending your soil to fix this as, in some cases it could be that they are there but the soil is too cold, too wet or too acidic or alkaline to release

Frozen lettuce probably won't recover.

the nutrients. Consider having your soil tested. Trace elements only need to be in the soil in small quantities and even the Nitrogen, Potassium and Phosphorus can be overdone and it is much harder to fix over-fertilised soil.

❋ Some problems will be showing more than one symptom.

❋ This isn't a comprehensive list of all possible problems, but should help you to begin the process of understanding what could be wrong. If you are unsure ask an expert in your area.

❋ For more information about common pests and diseases check out pages 84–90.

STEP ONE
Look closely to see what you can see – pay attention to under the leaves for tiny problems

Your problem will either be:
❋ a colour issue with the leaves
❋ involve spots or patches
❋ have holes
❋ the plant could be deformed in some way
❋ concern visible bugs
❋ have something to do with the fruit or flowers

STEP TWO
Decide which group best fits your problem

STEP THREE
From the group you have chosen go through the list to find out what could be the possible cause for your problem

Plants left in pots too long can be get stunted. All of these plants were sown at the same time 5 months ago.

STEP FOUR
Investigate possible solutions to your problem based on what is available in your area, or which solution suits your gardening style.

FLOWER AND FRUIT

NUTRIENTS	PESTS	DISEASE	ENVIRONMENT
POOR FRUIT SET			
			Too cold
			Too hot
			Lack of bees
			Wrong variety for time of year
BOLTING			
			Fluctuating temperatures
			Too dry
			Not enough organic matter
			Brassicas – soil too soft
TOO MANY MALE FLOWERS			
Plants hungry			Too cold
			Not bright enough
			Too early in season
ROTTING FRUIT			
Blossom End Rot – lack of available calcium		Grey Mould – Botrytis	Irregular watering
		Brown patches – Late Blight in Solanaceae	
HOLES			
	Caterpillars		
POOR FLAVOUR			
Too much nitrogen			
DISCOLOURATION			
			Too much sun – green shoulders
			Sunburn – crispy brown patches
SPLITING			
			Irregular watering
FLOWERS NOT SETTING			
			Too hot
			Too cold
			Too dry

LEAF COLOUR

NUTRIENTS	PESTS	DISEASE	ENVIRONMENT
YELLOW			
Nitrogen deficiency	Mites		Overwatered
Potassium deficiency			
Phosphorus deficiency			
Magnesium deficiency			
Sulphur deficiency			
Zinc deficiency			
Manganese deficiency			
Copper deficiency			
Iron deficiency			
BROWN			
Magnesium deficiency			Wind burn
Manganese deficiency			Frost damage
Iron deficiency			
RED			
Nitrogen deficiency			
Magnesium deficiency			
PURPLE			
Potassium deficiency			
BLUE			
Potassium deficiency			
SILVER			
	Thrips		
MOTTLED			
Copper deficiency	Mites	Virus	
Zinc deficiency			
STREAKY			
		Virus	

SPOTS OR PATCHES

NUTRIENTS	PESTS	DISEASE	ENVIRONMENT

SPOTS

Small concentric brown spots that grow bigger – Early Blight

Water-soaked spots that dry and crack – Leaf Spot

Small black spots – Leaf Spot

Orange spots – Rust

Circular spots on old cabbage leaves – Cabbage Ring Spot

Irregular shaped spots with halo – Bacterial Blight

PATCHES

Brown patches on leaves, stem and fruit in Solanaceae – Late Blight

Crispy brown patches – sunburn

Brown patches on leaves – Botrytis

FUZZ

Soft fuzzy white on stems and rotting – Sclerotinia

White fuzzy speckles on leaves – Powdery Mildew

Grey fuzzy rotting leaves and fruit – Grey Mould, Botrytis

Grey or purple fuzzy patches – Downy Mildew

BUGS

NUTRIENTS	PESTS	DISEASE	ENVIRONMENT

SMALL

Clusters of tiny green,
black, yellow or grey bugs
– aphids / greenfly – often
accompanied by ants

Tiny white flying bugs –
white fly

Clamped to underside of
leaf – Scale insects

Mites

MEDIUM

Caterpillars

Slugs

Green Vegetable Bugs

Snails

LARGE

Rats

Mice

Birds

Small children

Un-Gardeners

HOLES

NUTRIENTS	PESTS	DISEASE	ENVIRONMENT
HOLES IN FRUIT			
	Caterpillars		
HOLES IN LEAVES			
	Caterpillars		
	Slugs		
	Snails		
TUNNELS IN CARROTS			
	Carrot fly		

DEFORMED

NUTRIENTS	PESTS	DISEASE	ENVIRONMENT
WILTING			
		White mould – Sclerotinia	Soil too wet
		Bacterial wilt – affects Solanaceae family	Soil too dry
			Too hot
UNEVEN OR STUNTED GROWTH			
Boron deficiency		Brassica Club Root	Irregular watering
ROLLED LEAVES			
	Caterpillars		Temperature fluctuation
DISTORTED			
Molybdenum deficiency	Sap sucking insects	Virus	Herbicide over spray
	Thrips		
	Leaf Miner – thin white curly lines in leaves		
EXCESSIVE LEAF GROWTH			
Too much nitrogen			

TAKE NOTES

Taking notes while you garden throughout the growing season is really important to help you grow as a gardener. The forms provided throughout the book and here at the back, are a great start and a guide to what will be useful to record or you can keep notes in a large notebook or on your computer. Whichever way you take notes, just make sure you do. You'll thank yourself for it in the long run.

Garden Plan

Designing your garden is important for two reasons:
1. So you give the plants the best space so they grow well.
2. So you have a record for your crop rotation for seasons to come.

The grid provided can be used as scaled down metre squares marked out in bold with half and quarter metres marked out within the bold squares.

Make sure you record the date and where North is.

Planting out the garden.

Germination Record

Keeping notes of which seeds you have sown, how many and when they pop up is a great record to have to refer to in seasons to come and helps you to keep track of what you have going on. Seed sowing time can be hectic.

Harvest Record

It is all very well to grow all sorts of different things, however if you don't like how they taste or there wasn't a lot to harvest, then there isn't a lot of point growing them.

And on the other hand, if you grow something that is an absolute favourite, if you don't jot it down somewhere there is a high chance you will forget.

It also helps to keep a note of how prolific each crop was, to decide if it is worth growing again or not. Or even so you can compare it to the cost of produce in the store to determine just how much money your garden has saved you over the growing season.

Room For More

If you need more space to jot down what you have done each month, there is a place here. You can never take too many notes.

Seeds List

It is helpful to keep a record of your seeds and when they can be sown, to make it easy to plan your garden and ensure you don't forget to plant something important.

Each time you add new seeds to your collection, jot down the details, this can also help prevent ending up with more than one packet of your favourite things.

It can be helpful to keep a copy of your list in your seed tin so you can keep it all in one convenient place.

Things To Do Differently

Often when you are working away in the garden, an idea will come to you, or you see something that isn't quite working. It is a good idea to write this down as often the time to make the change is months away and easily forgotten and you are doomed to make the same mistakes again.

Weather Record

It is a good idea to keep a record of the weather you experience in your garden so in seasons to come you have an idea of what to expect from each month.

Take the time to write down for the week:

✳ The highest and lowest temperatures
✳ How much rain you had
✳ If it was really windy and which direction
✳ When frosts or snow occurred
✳ Anything unusual like a big storm or excessive flooding.

GARDEN PLAN

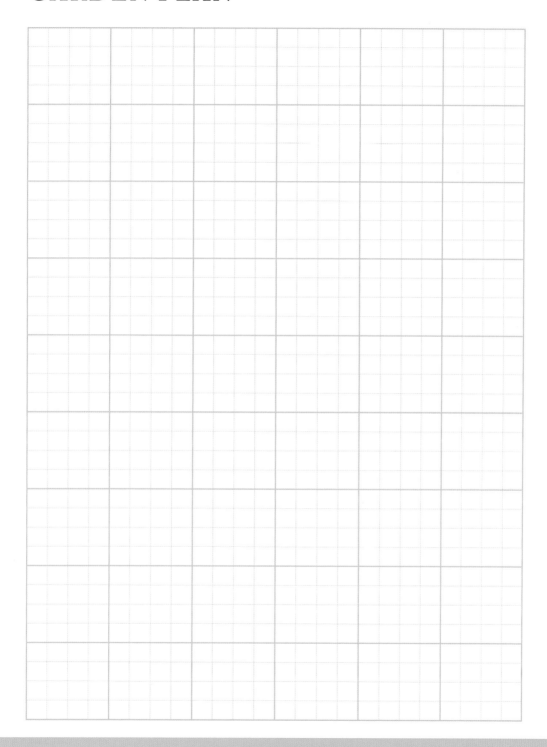

GERMINATION RECORD

DATE	SEED	NUMBER SOWN	DATE GERMINATED	NUMBER GERMINATED	DATE 1ST TRANSPLANT

DATE 2ND TRANSPLANT	INTO THE GARDEN	HARVEST DUE	COMMENTS

HARVEST RECORD

VARIETY	DATE OF FIRST HARVEST	HOW DID IT TASTE?

HOW MUCH DID YOU GET? Note each amount you harvest	TOTAL AMOUNT

ROOM FOR MORE

LATE WINTER

EARLY SPRING

MID-SPRING

LATE SPRING

EARLY SUMMER

MID-SUMMER

ROOM FOR MORE

LATE SUMMER

EARLY AUTUMN

MID-AUTUMN

LATE AUTUMN

EARLY WINTER

MID-WINTER

SEED LIST

VEGETABLE	VARIETY	EXPIRY DATE	SOWING DATES

THINGS TO DO DIFFERENTLY

WEATHER RECORD

TEMPERATURE		RAINFALL	FROST OR SNOW?	WINDY?	ANYTHING UNUSUAL
HIGH	LOW				
LATE WINTER					
EARLY SPRING					
MID-SPRING					
LATE SPRING					
EARLY SUMMER					
MID-SUMMER					

TEMPERATURE		RAINFALL	FROST OR SNOW?	WINDY?	ANYTHING UNUSUAL
HIGH	LOW				
LATE SUMMER					
EARLY AUTUMN					
MID-AUTUMN					
LATE AUTUMN					
EARLY WINTER					
MID-WINTER					

INDEX

UK £16.99   US $24.99